# GARDENING HACKS

## 300+ Time and Money Saving Hacks

## Jon VanZile

ADAMS MEDIA

NEW YORK   LONDON   TORONTO   SYDNEY   NEW DELHI

Adams Media
An Imprint of Simon & Schuster, Inc.
100 Technology Center Drive
Stoughton, MA 02072

First Adams Media trade paperback
edition April 2021

ADAMS MEDIA and colophon are
trademarks of Simon & Schuster.

For information about special
discounts for bulk purchases, please
contact Simon & Schuster Special
Sales at 1-866-506-1949 or
business@simonandschuster.com.

The Simon & Schuster Speakers
Bureau can bring authors to your
live event. For more information or
to book an event contact the Simon
& Schuster Speakers Bureau at
1-866-248-3049 or visit our website
at www.simonspeakers.com.

Interior design by Julia Jacintho
Illustrations by Alaya Howard

Manufactured in the
United States of America

3 2024

Library of Congress Cataloging-in-
Publication Data has been applied for.

ISBN 978-1-5072-1581-4
ISBN 978-1-5072-1582-1 (ebook)

# CONTENTS

# INTRODUCTION

Do you struggle to keep houseplants alive? Want to expand your current garden to include a wider variety of plants? Or maybe you've scrolled through *Pinterest* boards of immaculate gardens or interiorscapes and felt inspired to re-create the look in your own home. Perhaps you long to eat your own homegrown vegetables or arrange a vase of flowers you grew from seed.

No matter what your gardening question is, *Gardening Hacks* is your answer! With more than three hundred simple hacks, this book is your garden gate to less work, less expense, and more creativity in your garden, whether you're maintaining a vast veggie patch outside or a few plants inside your apartment. You'll find tips for how to feed and water your plants, keep pests away, and simply make gardening easier. You'll also discover dozens of longer DIY projects that solve specific garden problems or offer new ways of doing old things. Interested in building a space-saving tower for strawberries, onions, or potatoes? Looking for the best way to produce healthy seedlings or directions on how to create a hanging moss ball? Want to learn more about the numerous ways you can transform old 2-liter bottles into everything from terrariums to hanging gardens to hydroponic watering systems? *Gardening Hacks* has you covered with simple, easy-to-understand instructions.

In addition to offering practical tips on how to save money and effort in your garden, *Gardening Hacks* also supports environmentally friendly gardening principles. Many of the hacks are focused on reducing chemical use, employing time-tested organic gardening principles, and working *with* your environment instead of against it to create beautiful, natural settings.

So, whether you're counting down the days to harvest or looking for ways to finally master houseplants, grab your spade and dig in....The garden is open.

# HOW TO USE THIS BOOK

If you're looking for time-saving ideas, money-saving tips, and tricks for avoiding common hassles in your garden, you've come to the right place. Packed with more than three hundred hacks, this book can help you do everything from planting seeds to building a vertical vegetable garden to interiorscaping your home.

The material is organized into five chapters, each covering specific topics:

- Seeds, seedlings, and cuttings

- Container gardening

- Outdoor gardening

- Indoor gardening

- Tools, pests, and harvesting

Throughout the book, you'll find short and simple techniques that you can implement quickly, often with materials you already have around the house. Also included in each chapter are longer, DIY-style garden projects, which have been simplified so you can complete most in an afternoon. You might be surprised by how many ways you can use old 2-liter bottles in your garden, or the myriad uses for old newspaper and cardboard, glass bottles, old tires, extra building materials like cinder blocks or bricks, and even old appliances. Anything you don't have around the house should be available in a local garden center or big-box home-improvement store. This includes inexpensive materials like PVC, potting soil, fertilizer, all types of containers, garden tools, and almost anything else.

You can read the book from cover to cover, or browse and sample hacks here and there based on your interests and needs at any given moment. See what catches your imagination or sparks a new idea!

Here are a few tips to get the most from this book:

1. **Start with a general idea of what you want to work on.** If you're looking for the most effective ways to sprout seeds for your spring garden, for example, focus on the hacks that will work with your growing environment and specific plants.

2. **Keep an open mind.** There's no single "right" way to do anything. This book is all about trying new things while making gardening easier, less expensive, and less strenuous, no matter how you do it. Even if you're an experienced gardener, you might find a new way to do something you've been doing for years, or perhaps a clever way to recycle materials you already have sitting around the house. If you're just starting out growing things, you'll also be relieved to find that you don't need to know Latin to get the most from this book. The concepts and ideas presented here don't require an in-depth knowledge of horticultural concepts. The only limit is your imagination.

3. **Enjoy yourself!** Gardening is a fun, relaxing experience, so make the most of it. Don't get bogged down with making things look perfect or worrying about that one seed that didn't sprout. Simply live in the moment and appreciate your connection to the earth and the many beautiful and nourishing forms it can take.

Happy gardening!

# Chapter 1

# SEEDS, SEEDLINGS, AND CUTTINGS

## 1

## Loosen and fluff soil before planting (even in containers) to encourage strong root growth.

Plants rely on their roots for a steady supply of oxygen, water, and nutrients, so what's happening underground in your garden is just as important as what's going on above ground. To give your plants the best chance of thriving, plant them in loose, well-tilled, or turned soil. For small patches, you can turn over dirt with a shovel. Larger gardens might require a tiller (or a lot of help!). This is also true for your container plants. Unlike their in-ground cousins, container plants can't just send roots farther out if they need more water or air. Keeping the soil in your containers from compacting will help keep your plants robust.

## 2

## Nick large seeds before planting to speed up germination.

Before you plant large seeds, gently nick their outer shells with a needle or sharp blade. Seeds are designed to be very tough—in many cases, they need to survive being eaten by an animal, passing unscathed through a digestive tract, and then being naturally sown. That's why seeds are covered by a tough protective coating that only gets tougher when the seed is dried and stored. Gently nicking the seed coat makes it easier for water to penetrate the seed so it will germinate faster. Be careful, however, not to damage the delicate embryo inside.

## 3

# Make papier-mâché seed pots from newspaper.

These papier-mâché cups are great for slow-germinating seeds like peppers. To create a papier-mâché cup, shred about ten sheets of non-glossy newsprint, then soak the shredded paper in about 2 quarts of water for a few days. (The paper will partly disintegrate...this is fine.) Stir the newspaper until it forms a pulp with the consistency of oatmeal. Next drain off the remaining water from the pulp and add about 3 tablespoons of flour, mixing in the flour until the pulp forms a ball with the consistency of clay. Tear off chunks of the pulp mix and press it into standard muffin containers with your fingers, forming small cups. Let the tin sit out to dry for two or three days, or put it in a very low oven for a few minutes, until the cups are dry and sturdy. These durable little cups can be planted intact with your seedlings.

## 4

# Attach your germination records to seed packets.

No matter how you do it, record keeping is essential to becoming a better gardener...but how many of us keep organized and detailed plant journals (kudos if you're one of those gardeners who does!)? Try this tip to make record keeping easy: Write down germination information on a notecard, including how many days to germination, the date, and information such as germination rate and temperature. Then tape this notecard to the back of your seed packet. Next year, when it comes time to plant again, you'll be grateful to yourself when you can quickly locate everything you need to know to have a successful year.

# 5

## Save money by starting your seeds in cardboard tubes.

Looking for a clever way to recycle those old toilet paper tubes? Try using them as seed-starting containers. They're basically free, plus they are biodegradable so you can "plant" them directly in their final location without the stress of transplanting your seedlings. To make a toilet paper–tube planter, cut a standard-sized toilet paper tube in half, then make four cuts, about 1" long each, in one end. Fold and tuck the resulting flaps over themselves to create a bottom for the pot, then fill it with seedling starter soil and sow your seeds. Once the seeds are planted, place the little pots in a snug container and water normally. Be careful when you're ready to plant—the soggy cardboard will be ready to disintegrate, which is exactly what you want so your seedling can send out roots.

## 6

## Create quick paper pots from scrap paper and newspapers.

If you prefer a method that's faster and easier than papier-mâché, you can easily make biodegradable, organic seedling pots from a few sheets of newspaper. Cut a 10"-or-so square of newspaper sheets (use at least five sheets), then wrap them around a spice jar as a mold. To create the pot bottom, fold the newspaper around the bottom of the jar and use a bit of tape or a drop of glue to secure the paper. Gently slide the tube off the jar and stand it upright, then fold the top ½" or so over itself. This will help hold the paper pot together and give it some strength. Once that's done, fill the pot with soil and plant. Be aware, however, that these pots won't last long before the newspaper degrades, so stick with fast-germinating seeds like lettuce.

## 7

## Count your nodes!

Taking cuttings is one of the best ways to increase your plant stock. It's easy and fast and yields plants that are genetically identical to their parent plants. But there's a trick if you want to get it right: Make sure you're counting nodes. Nodes are the areas where branches or leaves emerge from the main stem. In general, you want to make sure you have at least two viable nodes in the water or soil with every cutting. It also helps to take cuttings from new growth that's still supple. This makes it easier to strip off the nodes you need and increases your odds of success.

# 8

# Recycle 2-liter bottles to create a mini "greenhouse."

Empty 2-liter bottles have almost endless uses when it comes to starting seeds, including making self-contained "greenhouses" for your seedlings. While it is possible to just add soil and water, then sow your seeds and cover them, if you take a few extra steps, you can help prevent damping off (seedlings dying or failing).

## Materials:

- 2 (2-liter) plastic bottles
- Soil
- Seeds
- Tape

## Instructions:

1. Cut 5"–6" off the bottom of one bottle, leaving the spout intact.

2. Cut the second bottle in half crosswise, but not all the way through—just enough to flip it open.

3. Insert the top of the first bottle upside down in the bottom half of the second bottle.

4. Add soil to the upside-down bottle and sow your seeds directly in the soil. Water the seedlings, but don't soak the soil.

5. Reassemble the second bottle and tape it shut. It will look a little like an hourglass, with an upside-down bottle top full of soil enclosed in it.

6. Put the top back onto the second bottle and put it in a warm, bright place, but not in direct sunlight.

7. The idea here is to create natural drainage for your seeds as they sprout and grow. Excess water will collect in the bottom of your greenhouse, only to be soaked up when it's needed.

## 9

# Save your tomato and pepper seeds to plant next year.

If you liked what you grew last season, why not plan ahead to grow it again next year? Fortunately, some of the easiest seeds to save are also the most popular vegetables:

- **Peppers:** Choose fully ripe peppers to save for seeds. Cut the pepper in half and shake the seeds onto a plate or dish. Let them sit out for a week or so until they are fully dry, then store them in a cool, dry place for up to three years.

- **Tomatoes:** Tomato seeds are covered with a natural protective gel, so you need to remove it via fermentation. Start with ripe fruit and gently squeeze the "guts" (gel and seeds) into a small jar. Cover the jar with a paper towel and let it sit at room temperature for three days. Discard any floating seeds and rinse the seeds and gel in a strainer under water. Place the seeds on paper towels to dry for about two weeks.

# 10

## Use citrus rinds as organic seedling containers.

Here's a simple hack that is eco-friendly and lovely to look at: Instead of tossing your citrus peels, convert them into seedling containers. Lemons especially work great. Simply cut the top third off a lemon, then juice or scoop out the flesh and pulp. The resulting rind is a perfect container! Just fill it with a little seedling soil, add your seeds, and water carefully. You can keep the citrus "container" in a small bowl or empty egg carton. Since the rind is organic, it will slowly deteriorate as your seeds sprout and begin to grow. When it's finally time to transplant, just bury the rind, so you never have to disturb the seedlings' fragile roots.

# 11

## Use squeezable condiment containers to dose fertilizer.

Feeding seedlings is a delicate process. In general, you don't want to add fertilizer right after they sprout, because it might damage the tender shoots. When you do start fertilizing a few days later, be careful with the amount and type of fertilizer. One of the better organic fertilizers for seedlings is fish emulsion, which is wonderful stuff for plants but smells exactly how you'd think: like rotting fish. To help control the odor and very precisely dose the stinky brew, try buying some small squeezable condiment containers and filling them with the fertilizer solution. When it comes time to feed your seedlings, a single squirt is all you'll need.

## 12

## Make DIY "greenhouses" from plastic bins.

Looking to get an early start on your medium or large veggie garden? Create portable "greenhouses" by putting pots inside large, clear bins from your local big-box store. You can use any size container you need, as long as it's big enough to hold all your pots. And if you buy a bin with flaps to close the top, there's no need to punch any holes in the container itself—you can leave the flaps propped open to ensure good airflow, or close them to hold in heat. This simple DIY greenhouse won't make any mess and is easy to carry outside at planting time, plus the bins are large enough to hold a bunch of small pots. Just one word of caution: Be careful when you water not to add more water than your plants can soak up from the bottom. If you do see standing water, try to pour it off or remove it using a ladle or turkey baster.

## 13

## Soak seeds for 24 hours before planting them, to encourage growth.

While it's easy enough to drop a seed into a starting mix and hope for the best, soaking your seeds before planting can increase their germination rate and speed up their sprouting time. Soaking your seeds for up to 24 hours before you plant them helps break down the tough outer shell and softens the seed before planting. To soak seeds, simply place them in clean water and leave them alone. Remember to label your jars or soaking bowls so you don't forget which seeds are which!

## 14

## Repurpose your eggshells into seed containers.

Eggshells are a versatile friend to gardeners, but here's one idea you might not have considered: Start your seedlings directly in eggshells. This idea is exactly as simple as it sounds: Save eggshells that are broken in half, fill them with a little bit of seedling soil, and sow your seeds directly in the shells. As with any closed container that lacks drainage, be careful with your watering. For easy storage, save the egg carton your eggs came in and start twelve seedlings at once. At planting time, plant the shell and seedling together—the shell will gradually break down and provide some calcium to your plant. One note: This method works best for smaller seedlings like herbs, which don't require as much growing room.

## 15

## Plant seeds in paper cups.

Transplant shock is always a risk when it comes time to move your seedlings from their original containers to their final destination. If you're not interested in making biodegradable containers on your own, here's another easy approach: Use paper cups for your seedlings. Poke a few holes in the bottoms of regular paper cups, fill them with seedling mix, and plant. Ideally, look for non-wax-coated cups that will disintegrate easily, so when it comes time to plant, you can just bury the whole cup without disturbing your seedlings' roots. Paper cups have another advantage too: You can write on them, so you'll know which plant is which!

## 16

### Recycle old K-Cup containers into seedling containers.

K-Cups are convenient, but they're not very environmentally friendly, since every cup of coffee creates a new piece of disposable plastic. Instead of throwing yours away, why not convert them into seedling containers for your herb garden? Just poke a hole in the bottom for drainage, fill with seedling starter soil, and plant directly in the cup. Remember to label your pots with a Sharpie or other permanent marker so you keep track of your seedlings! You'll have to transplant your seedlings from their little K-Cups at transplanting time, but you'll have the satisfaction of knowing you got one more use out of them.

## 17

### Train your seedlings and transplants with soldering wire.

Training plants is necessary sometimes if you have limited growing space or if you want to achieve a certain look (think bonsai, which are extensively trained). If you want to train a plant to grow into a certain shape, it's best to start when the plant is still young and supple. You can use specialized plant-training wire to do this, or you can cut your costs down and use highly malleable soldering wire. This product is widely available in hardware stores, easy to cut and bend, and strong enough to hold its shape. Also, there's no reason to worry about lead—soldering wire no longer contains lead, so it's safe to use.

## 18

# Use honey to strengthen your cuttings.

Honey is one of nature's more miraculous ideas. It's naturally anti-bacterial and antimicrobial and full of enzymes that stimulate plant growth. If you like to take cuttings of your plants, instead of buying an expensive rooting hormone, you can use honey instead. Here's how:

- Using a sharp knife, take a cutting of your plant using a diagonal cut. Choose a cutting that has at least three sets of leaves, then trim off the bottom set.
- Dip the cutting in honey, then let the excess drip off.
- Gently plant the cutting in moist seedling soil.
- Place the cutting in a warm, humid area until new growth emerges.

## 19

# Add LED grow lights to your seedling-growing space.

One of the great challenges facing indoor gardeners is the lack of light—and this is especially true if you're trying to get your seedlings going indoors. Even on a bright windowsill, indoor seedlings often don't get enough light, so they stretch out, resulting in weak stems. Solve this problem with simple and inexpensive LED grow lights (these are different than the light strips used for heat). There are many types of LED grow lights on the market today. Look for LED lights in the red and blue spectrum that are portable and can be repurposed when you're not growing seedlings.

# Create a cheap seedling heat mat with LED strip lights.

You can improve your germination rate and time to germination by using a dedicated heat mat under your seed-starting trays. Skip buying expensive systems and use standard LED light strips instead. This project can be as simple or as complicated as you like: You can fasten the strips to a wooden board and rest your seedling trays on the strip, or you can simply coil the light strip on a surface and set your seedling containers on the lights. Don't worry—LED lights don't put off enough heat to burn your seedlings, but they do emit just enough heat to encourage healthy germination and growth. After you're done, you can repurpose the LED light strip as decorative lights!

## 21

# Make your own seed tape.

Seed tape is the ultimate word in precision planting. It allows you to place precise numbers of seeds into furrows, perfectly spaced apart. Unfortunately, commercial seed tape has some pretty serious drawbacks, including its expense and the fact that it can be hard to find. Instead, you can make your own seed tape with easy-to-find materials.

## Instructions:

1. Select your seeds and check the seed packet to determine how far apart the adult plants should be placed.

2. Lay out a strip of toilet paper or paper towel several inches wide.

3. Mix flour and water in a 2:1 ratio to create seed glue. The glue should be thick and not too moist—you don't want your seeds to sprout early!

4. Measure along the strip of toilet paper and make dots with a marker or pen to show where the seeds should go. The distance between your dots should be the distance your adult plants will ultimately need.

5. Put a small drop of seed glue on each dot, then place a seed into each drop of glue.

6. When you're done with the whole strip, place a few drops of glue along the edge of the paper and fold it over to protect the seeds.

7. Let the tape sit out for a few hours so the glue dries fully.

8. Store the seed tape by rolling it around a paper towel or toilet paper tube.

9. When you're ready to plant, dig a trough and unspool the seed tape into the trough. Water the strip gently and wait. The tape and glue will both quickly degrade, so your seeds can sprout easily.

## 22

## Sprout seeds on a paper towel to be sure they're viable.

This easy sprouting method can be done indoors, with minimal equipment or space. Simply moisten a square of paper towel, then sprinkle your seeds on the towel. Fold the paper towel over the seeds, then place it in a baggie or a sealed plastic food container. You don't want to soak the paper towel—seeds need only a moist environment to sprout. The germination time depends on the type of seed (check the seed packet for information), but generally, most seeds will sprout within 2–7 days. While you're waiting, check the paper towel daily to make sure it's continuously moist; you can mist it if it starts to dry out. Once the seeds are sprouted, carefully transfer them to the planting container.

## 23

### Use coconut coir pellets for seeds.

If you've never germinated your seeds with coconut coir pellets, you're missing out on one of the easiest, least expensive methods to get your garden started. These little discs, made of compressed coconut coir in a delicate net, are widely available in garden centers and big-box stores. All you need to do is add water and let them expand. Once they've expanded, seeds can be easily planted through a hole in the top of the netting, and the pellets can be lined up snugly in a tray. Coconut coir naturally retains water, so you're less likely to over- or underwater, and the little pellets can be planted whole when it comes time to transplant.

## 24

### Mix small seeds with sand when planting to spread them out.

Planting very small seeds like carrot seeds can be tricky—it's easy to end up piling your seeds in one place, only to thin the seedlings out later and destroy dozens of viable plants. To prevent this, try mixing your tiny seedlings with very fine, dry sand before sowing. Playground sand is a great option, but make sure you're using clean sand that isn't loaded with contaminants and weeds. Pour your mix of seeds and sand into a saltshaker and use this to spread seeds evenly in prepared troughs. This will ensure your plants are spread more evenly, cutting down on wasted seeds.

# 25

## Make your own soil blocks.

Soil blocks, or small cubes of compressed soil, are a convenient and effective way to start seedlings. To make your own soil blocks, use a can opener to remove both ends of a 6-ounce tomato paste can. For your soil plunger, buy a large dowel that fits inside the empty can, or you can screw one of the can tops to a thin dowel. Create a seed-starting mix by combining sphagnum moss and water until it forms a very moist, thick mixture. Holding the can upright on a flat surface, fill it halfway with the moist mixture, then compress with your plunger. Use enough pressure to form a tight, well-formed plug. Completed blocks can be pushed gently from the can with your plunger. To plant in the blocks, form a small hole in the top and drop your seeds in. Soil blocks can be spaced apart in a tray and gently watered.

# 26

## Water seedlings from the bottom to prevent collapse.

The most dangerous thing you'll do to seedlings is also one of the most important: watering. Overwatered seedlings are prone to collapse, which can set you back weeks on your garden planning. The best way to avoid this is to simply water your seeds from below by pouring water into the seedling tray and giving them a few minutes to soak up what they need. After about 10 minutes, drain the excess water off so they aren't sitting in water. An added benefit to watering from below: Roots are encouraged to fill the container as they reach for water.

## 27
## Mix up your own seedling starter soil.

Seeds and seedlings are highly sensitive to fertilizer, competition from weeds, and too much moisture, so it's always best to start your seedlings in a special soil mix. While you can buy seedling mix, you can save money by making your own from peat moss or coconut coir plus inorganic elements like perlite and vermiculite. Mix peat moss or coconut coir with perlite and vermiculite in a 2:1:1 proportion. The moss or coconut coir will provide a growing medium, while the perlite and vermiculite increase drainage and add structure. When working with perlite and vermiculite, always follow safety instructions—breathing the dust can be harmful. Although adding fertilizer is not recommended, you can mix in a few tablespoons of worm castings per gallon of mix to give the seedlings a boost.

## 28
## Create a seedling terrarium from an old aquarium.

Give your old, empty aquariums new life by converting them into seedling terrariums. Like the original Wardian cases early European botanists used to transport plant specimens, terrariums are perfect environments for delicate plants. The glass walls allow in plenty of light, or you can use the original cover and install a grow light on it. Because it's a closed system with no drainage, you'll need to add a layer of gravel to the bottom of the aquarium before adding your seedling starter mix. Or you can set small pots directly into the aquarium. The resulting environment will be warm, humid, and protected...the ideal environment for sprouting seeds and getting seedlings started.

# 29

## Make DIY "greenhouse hot caps" from 2-liter bottles.

If you want to start your seeds outside but are worried it's still a little cold, here's another use for empty 2-liter bottles: Use them to make "hot caps" for your pots. Hot caps are basically mini greenhouses that protect individual plants. To make your own, cut the bottom off a 2-liter bottle and place the top over your plant. You can leave the cap on as long as the plant is not in direct sunlight—you don't want to cook your seedlings. A typical 2-liter bottle has a diameter of 4", so these are perfect for small containers. You can also put the bottle tops on the ground for direct-sown seedlings. Always use clear bottles to allow for maximum light. At watering time, gently water from the top, or you can remove the homemade hot cap and water as normal.

# 30

## Upcycle a takeout container into a microgreen garden.

Instead of buying expensive microgreens, why not repurpose clear, plastic clamshell-style takeout containers into microgreen gardens? This easy trick yields a constant supply of delicious microgreens. All you need is a clean, clear plastic clamshell; seed-starting mix; and microgreen seeds.

### Instructions:

1. Wash and sterilize your clamshell with a regular bleach cleanser, rinsing well.

2. Fill with 1"–2" of seedling mixture, depending on how deep it is.

3. Sow a dense single layer of seeds into the soil.

4. Gently water.

5. Cover with lid.

6. Keep in a bright place away from direct sunlight and wait for your microgreens to sprout!

## 31

## Record plant names and pictures on your phone so you remember what you planted where.

Planting time is a hopeful time—and sometimes a time of gentle self-deception. "Sure," you think, "I'll remember what I planted here! How could I forget?" Fast-forward a few weeks to when your garden has grown in, and you're standing in front of rows of seedlings wondering what's where. Here's a simple trick: When you plant, stand back and take a picture of your garden on a smartphone, then label the picture with the text tool, noting what plants are where. This way, instead of guessing later on what you planted, you can pull up the image on your phone and have an instant map to your own garden.

## 32

## Take time-stamped pictures of your seedlings to track your progress.

Keeping track of your planting times, germination times, watering and feeding schedules, and growth makes it easy to refine your growing methods from year to year, so you can master the particular details of your unique microclimate and your favorite plants. To streamline your record keeping, take regular photos of your plants. Label photos with dates and relevant details and store them somewhere in your photo library—you'll thank yourself next year.

## 33

# Sow your seeds in the winter to prepare for spring.

Winter sowing is a great trick for gardeners who aren't interested in investing in the equipment to start their seeds inside in early spring, or who don't have room for a full-fledged seed-starting operation inside. The idea behind winter sowing is simple—you create mini greenhouses from common household containers (standard milk jugs are the best), then plant your seeds in early winter and leave them outside all winter. When the weather warms up, the seeds will sprout in their protected DIY greenhouses and grow naturally until transplant time.

## Materials:

- Gallon plastic milk jugs (no caps needed)
- Hole punch or power drill
- Potting soil
- Cold-hardy seeds (perennials, herbs, or fall-sown vegetables)
- Duct tape

## Instructions:

1. Start by cutting the milk jugs nearly in half crosswise, so you can flip them open.
2. Punch or drill small drainage holes in the bottoms of the containers.
3. Fill the containers with 4" of potting soil.

4. Sow your seeds, burying at the recommended depth.

5. Water the soil.

6. Flip the jugs closed and fasten with duct tape.

7. Move the jugs outside in freezing weather so they don't sprout early.

8. Wait until spring!

9. When the weather warms up, your plants will sprout on their own. At this point, you can begin watering and caring for them like any other seedling. Transplant into your garden when they have outgrown their containers.

## 34

# Store seed packets in trading-card sleeves to keep them organized.

If you're a regular seed buyer, you probably have half-filled packets of seeds lying around, waiting for the next season or the next time you want to grow that particular plant again. Here's a great way to keep all those seed packets safe and organized: Store the envelopes in a three-ring binder filled with trading-card sleeves. The clear plastic sleeves are the perfect size to slip seed packets into, and you can quickly and easily see exactly what you have. It's also helpful to date each packet, so you know how old the seeds are and which ones are approaching the end of their viability.

## 35
### Use shop lights as seedling lights.

Starting your seedlings inside is the best way to extend your growing season, but it can be challenging to provide enough light for your light-hungry seedlings. Fortunately, seedlings aren't too picky when it comes to types of light: You can grow excellent seedlings under standard fluorescent shop lights, with no need to buy a fancy seed-starting kit. Because these lights are cool burning, you can hang them just 1"–2" above your seedlings with no risk of burning your plants. For most types of seedlings, you should provide 24 hours of continuous light at first, so they'll grow faster and stronger. At the minimum, they should be left on 16 hours a day until the plants are ready to be moved outside.

## 36
### Space out plants in a grid using a muffin tin.

There's a bit of art and a bit of science to planting dense beds of herbs, veggies, and flowers. You want your plants spaced out just enough so they can grow well, but not so far that weeds can take over. If you want perfect spacing, try using an old muffin tin as a natural spacer. First, prepare your bed so the soil is ready and aerated, then push the muffin tin into the dirt to create perfectly spaced planting holes. Sow seeds into the holes, cover with more soil, and water. Voilà! When your plants emerge, they'll be spaced on a perfect grid.

## 37

## Use a fan to produce stronger seedlings.

There's a reason most plants produce abundant seeds: Nature is not a kind or gentle place for tender shoots. You can imagine how shocking it is for your pampered seedlings to be transferred from your protected indoor growing space to the outdoor garden. To make this transition easier on your seedlings, give your indoor seedlings a pretransplant workout with a simple fan. Directing a steady flow of air onto your tray of seedlings will toughen their stems, increase air circulation and help prevent damping off (seedlings dying or failing), and ease their transition outside. Just be careful not to blow your seedlings over! For the first week or so, you might have to gently stake them up with bamboo skewers.

## 38

## Save your old prescription bottles for seed storage.

If you're the type of gardener who buys more seeds than you could possibly plant, you're likely always looking for ways to store the extra seeds. Why not use your old prescription bottles? These little bottles are designed to protect what's inside from excess moisture and light, and they are childproof. To keep things organized, cut the front of the seed packet out and tape it to the prescription bottle, so you'll know exactly what's inside. Remember to write the date on the label so you'll know how old all your seeds are. Seeds in prescription bottles can be stored in a cool, dark place for years.

## 39

## Prop up seedlings with bamboo skewers.

Even with perfect light and good ventilation, some vigorous seedlings grow too fast for their own good. These fast growers can easily become top-heavy and tip over with the slightest breeze, causing you to lose some of your healthiest young plants. Here's a simple fix: Pick up some regular bamboo skewers from the supermarket. These are inexpensive and durable, and you can cut them to size. To prop up your seedlings, insert skewers directly into the soil around your plants. In many cases, you won't even have to tie the plant up—the skewers will form a little protective cage, providing just enough support to let your seedlings flourish. At transplant time, remove the skewers and plant as normal.

## 40

## Start rose cuttings in potatoes.

This trick probably dates back hundreds of years to when early settlers migrated from Europe to North America. The potatoes provided a ready source of nutrition for young plants, as well as plentiful moisture and enough structure to hold up for longer trips. To try this method, start with healthy rose cuttings and trim the cut end on an angle. Use a screwdriver that's slightly smaller than the rose stem to bore a hole into a regular potato, going almost all the way through the tuber. Push the rose into the hole so it's secure, then bury the potato and rose cutting in regular potting soil. Over time, the potato will rot, and roots will emerge. Your degree of success may vary with this trick, but if you have some extra rose cuttings, it's a fun way to increase your collection.

# 41

## Plant seeds in ice cream cones.

What's the second-best thing you can put into an ice cream cone? Seeds! Using ice cream cones is a cheap and fun way to start seedlings. All you need are cake ice cream cones with a flat bottom (not the hard sugar cones), seedling starter mix, and seeds. Poke a hole in the bottom of the cone, then fill it with soil like a regular container and sow the seed. These can be watered like normal containers, although it's best to water from the top so the cones don't disintegrate too fast. At planting time, bury the whole cone and seedling—the cone will deteriorate quickly, allowing the plant to grow into its adult size.

# 42

## Start seeds in cardboard egg containers.

The humble cardboard egg container makes an excellent planter for small seedlings and microgreens. These biodegradable cartons are the perfect size and material for seedlings. Just fill the empty carton with seedling starter mix, then sow seeds. Water carefully—the cardboard will soak up water and help keep your mix moist while the seeds sprout and grow. If you're transplanting, use kitchen shears to cut the individual "mini pots" apart and bury them with the seedlings. They'll quickly disintegrate, so your seedlings can grow to their full size.

# 43

## Grow your own "popcorn" from kernels.

Popcorn is a staple of movie night for a good reason: It's low calorie, tasty, and fun to cook. But did you realize those popping kernels are actually seeds? In fact, you can grow your own popcorn. Make sure you're using plain dried kernels that haven't been doused with added butter and salt, then follow these easy tips to start your own popcorn garden.

### Instructions:

1. Sow the kernels in the ground, burying them about 2" deep and about 8" apart. Sow when the soil temperature is about 60°F.

2. Mulch the soil.

3. Once the corn plants emerge, water regularly and fertilize. In about 120 days, you'll be able to pop your own corn.

## 44

## "Cook" away pests and problems in your spring planting beds.

In many parts of the country that don't have deep freezes, pests and microorganisms in garden beds are a real problem. These nasties can attack your newly transplanted plants and ruin your season before it gets started. If this sounds familiar, try this trick from professional growers: Cook the pests before you plant. This is actually much easier than it sounds. All you need is a roll of standard black landscaping plastic and some stakes. Simply stake the plastic over your entire garden bed, making sure it's completely covered, and leave the plastic in place for a week or two, hoping for sunny days. The sun will heat the black plastic and the soil beneath, killing bacteria and driving away many soilborne pests. When it comes time to plant, you can either plant directly through the plastic sheeting or remove it and plant as you normally would.

## 45

## Convert empty milk jugs into plant covers.

Early spring planting is a great way to get a jump on the season, but it has risks of its own: Chilly nights can kill your precious seedlings and set you back weeks. Instead of risking it all, save some of those old milk jugs and turn them into individual plant covers (also known as "cloches"). To create these simple cloches, cut the bottoms from the milk jugs and place the tops over your plants (with the caps off so there's good ventilation). You can water through the open cap as well as around the edges of the cloche. As an added bonus, the cloches will protect your tender and delicious seedlings from hungry pests, including deer and rabbits.

## 46

## Make DIY sleeves for your tree saplings.

Here's an easy way to protect your tree saplings from cute but voracious eaters: Make sleeves from large-diameter PVC pipe. You'll first need a length of large PVC pipe, about 4" or 5" in diameter and long enough that you can cut one 18" piece for every sapling. Using a hacksaw, cut one sleeve for every sapling, then drive it into the ground over your sapling to protect it. The tall, narrow sleeves will provide a few critical weeks or months of protection while your sapling grows.

## 47

### Expand your plant collection by taking cuttings.

Taking cuttings is an easy and inexpensive way to increase your plant collection, but it's not always easy to get cuttings to root. Here are a few tricks to help you succeed:

- Start with vines! Vines often readily root from cuttings.

- Take cuttings that have at least two nodes (where the leaves emerge from the stem).

- Use a sharp knife and cut the stem at an angle.

- Coat the cut end in rooting hormone, honey, or cinnamon.

- Plant in seedling starter mix.

- Place in a warm, bright, humid area like a bathroom.

- Depending on the plant, you should see new growth emerge within a few days to a few weeks. Voilà! You have a new plant.

# 48

## Make your own "seed bombs."

These little self-contained packets are not only a great way to spread wildflowers wherever they land; they're also a really cool craft project to involve your kids in. Once you've mixed up a few dozen of these balls, you'll have a great time "bombing" any local patch of dirt that would be brightened by flowers. Just throw a few seed bombs into a weedy patch and let rain do the rest.

### Materials:

- Newspaper or protective sheet
- Air-dry clay
- Potting soil
- A few packets of wildflower seeds

### Instructions:

1. Prepare your working area with newspaper or a protective sheet. This is messy!

2. In a large bowl, combine air-dry clay with some water and potting soil and mix until it forms the consistency of cookie dough, adding water or soil as necessary. You should be able to form wet clumps that stick together.

3. Mix the wildflower seeds into the clay and dirt mixture, spreading them evenly.

**4.** Form 1"–1½" balls with the mixture.

**5.** Spread the balls out on more newspaper or parchment paper to dry.

**6.** The finished seed bombs can be stored in a cool, dry place. Using them couldn't be simpler: Just toss seed bombs wherever you want to seed with wildflowers. Rain will disintegrate the clay and cause the seeds to sprout. Not all the bombs will sprout, but no worries! You can always make more.

## 49

## Protect your seedlings with cinnamon.

Cinnamon is more than delicious: This remarkable spice has multiple uses in the garden, including as an antifungal agent that can help protect your seedlings against the dreaded damping off (seedlings dying or failing). But before you go sprinkling cinnamon on all your plants, there are a few things you should know. First, there are several kinds of cinnamon sold under the single name of "cinnamon." According to studies, the most active antifungal cinnamon is the more expensive "true" cinnamon, which is often sold as Ceylon or Sri Lankan cinnamon. If you want to get the most action, dissolve a teaspoon or so in a pint of water before you use it. This will spread the cinnamon more evenly through the soil.

# 50

## Propagate succulents from their own leaves.

Succulents are some of the most popular indoor plants because they're tough, drought resistant, and slow growing. They're also incredibly easy to propagate from cuttings with no special equipment or technique. This works best with fleshy-leaf succulents like echeveria or jade plants.

### Instructions:

1. Gently snip full leaves from your succulent, getting as close to the stem as possible.

2. Let the leaf dry out for two or three days. Leave it on a counter or windowsill until a scab forms over the cut part.

3. Lay the leaves on a moist soil bed.

4. Mist them daily, keeping the soil moist but not saturated.

5. That's it! Depending on the time of year and type of succulent, it can take anywhere from 1–3 weeks for baby plants to appear. And don't be discouraged if not all your leaves sprout—it can take a while to get the hang of this technique, and even experienced growers don't expect a 100 percent success rate.

## 51

### Use tweezers to handle sprouted seeds.

Sprouting seeds on paper towels is a great way to guarantee that you're only planting viable seeds, but it's not without risk. Once a seed sprouts, or "tails," it's very fragile and vulnerable. If you break off the little white tail while transplanting the seed, that's the end of that plant. So, here's a simple way to protect your precious sprouted seeds: Use an old pair of tweezers to move them. Once you get the hang of it, you'll find yourself whisking sprouted seeds from their moist towel into soil without a second thought and no damage to your little sprout.

## 52

### Repurpose old screens as plant covers.

If you're the type of gardener who loves to grow tender leafy greens or sows your seeds directly into the ground, you already know you're not the only one who likes these delicate morsels. Rabbits and deer will come from far and wide to destroy your garden. Here's a clever idea to protect your seedlings: Repurpose old screens to create protective plant covers. To make it work, either build a raised "box" of two-by-fours around the bed, or make a wall of railroad ties or even cinder blocks. Lay the screens over the makeshift frame and fasten them with clamps or screws. You can water through the screen, while your unwanted visitors will be blocked from devouring your young plants.

## 53

# Make your own floating row covers to protect young plants.

Floating row covers are a simple and effective tool to protect your garden early in the season.

## Materials:

- Sturdy stakes or rebar (number of stakes will vary depending on the size of your bed)
- ½" flexible PVC tubing (length will vary depending on the size of your bed)
- Old sheets or row cover material
- Tent stakes or heavy stones

## Instructions:

1. Drive the stakes or rebar into the ground on either side of your growing bed, spacing them 18" apart and sticking up about a foot, until you've formed a border of stakes.

2. Slide the PVC over the rebar and bend it gently into an arc so you can slide the other end over the rebar on the other side of the row. Repeat with the remaining stakes. Lay a long piece of PVC across the top of your hoops and tie it in place. Drape your fabric over the hoops and stake it to the ground.

# 54

## Sow tiny seeds with a pepper shaker to make the most of them.

Sowing tiny seeds can be a tricky proposition. If you're not careful, you'll end up with clumps of plants you'll have to thin out later, or you'll end up losing lots of seeds to wind. Why not make things easier with a common household device that's perfectly suited to spreading small grains? An old pepper shaker is the ideal tool to help you spread tiny seeds evenly and with minimal waste. Just load the shaker up with seeds, dig your troughs, and scatter away.

# 55

## Start early, plant early, harvest more.

Why does the gardening season always seem too short? Even on good years, who hasn't nervously watched the weather for dreaded frost or cold snaps that will destroy ripening crops, or been forced to pick early? While you'll never be able to control the weather, you can take a few steps to maximize every decent day on the calendar:

- Start your seeds indoors! You don't need special equipment— old shop lights are enough to get started.
- Protect your seedlings with row covers, cloches, or hot caps.
- Keep your seedlings watered to protect their roots!

## 56

### Start your own lemon trees.

This fun experiment isn't really about growing your own lemons—after all, commercial lemon trees are usually grafted, and it's unlikely a lemon tree grown from seed would yield the same fruit you buy in a supermarket. But that shouldn't detract from the thrill of sprouting and growing a lemon on your own. To sprout a lemon seed, first remove the seeds from a lemon and wash them well, making sure to remove any pulp. You can plant the pips directly into seed-starting soil, water them gently, and put them in a warm spot—it's a good idea to plant a few at once, in case they don't germinate. The seeds should sprout in about two weeks. After that, keep your lemon tree in a bright, warm place and water regularly.

## 57

### Preheat your seedling mix to kill fungus.

The good news is that most store-bought seed-starting mix is sterile. The bad news is that if you like to make your own mix to save money, you can't be sure your raw ingredients aren't harboring one of the nasty fungi that cause damping off. To ensure your seedlings have every possible chance of success, try preheating your homemade seed-starting mix. Simply put the mixture into a preheated oven at 180°F for 30 minutes. When you're done, remove and let it cool before using.

## 58

# Bury the stems of tomato seedlings very deeply to grow big tomatoes.

Planting tomato seedlings is always hopeful—it means you can start looking forward to the harvest in a few short months. But this is also the time when tomato plants are the most vulnerable. Give yours an extra boost with this trick recommended by experts and experienced tomato growers: Strip off some bottom leaves so you can plant the stem deep in the ground. This means burying part of the stem that was previously above ground. Some growers even lay tomatoes sideways in shallow trenches so they can bury more stem. This works because the tomato stem will quickly sprout extra roots, allowing it to take up more water and nutrients faster so it can grow bigger.

## 59

# Take cuttings of outdoor plants to use inside.

Who says you can't grow "outside" plants inside? If you're looking for a source of new, inexpensive plants that are already used to your climate, don't forget the great outdoors. Next time you're trimming your shrubs or dividing bulbs or clumping plants, why not set aside a few cuttings or divisions for use as houseplants? You can treat the cuttings like any others, either starting them directly in soil or in water. Just remember: Your outdoor plants might have pests, so when you first bring something in, make sure to quarantine it away from other plants for a few weeks so you don't bring in pests to your regular houseplants.

# 60

## Train your transplants early and often.

There are lots of good reasons to train your plants to grow in a certain direction. Maybe you have a limited growing area, or maybe you want your adult plant to achieve a certain aesthetic appeal. Whatever your reason, if you want to make things easier on yourself, here's a tip: Start early, when your seedlings are strong enough to handle it but still supple enough to easily bend and shape. At this stage, you can train your plants with almost anything—a paper clip is plenty strong enough to bend a young branch on a small seedling. The benefits of starting early will pay off later when you won't have to stress your plant with heavy pruning or staking.

# 61

## Try planting unroasted coffee beans.

Coffee isn't just another plant—this small tropical bush is the source of the obsessively beloved beverage that fuels mornings the world over. But did you know coffee can be grown as a houseplant from green, unroasted beans? To grow your own, soak a handful of beans in a wide dish of water for 24 hours. The germination rate of unroasted beans is pretty low, so you'll need a decent-sized handful. Once you see sprouted beans, plant them just like any other seed. Remember, coffee is tropical, so it will thrive in warm, humid rooms with dappled light and steady moisture. Once the seedlings are established, you can grow your coffee like any other houseplant—and if you're really lucky, you might even harvest your own coffee beans.

# 62

## Try mushroom propagation.

You can grow popular strains of mushroom with some very basic equipment. First, pick what type of mushroom you want to grow. Oyster mushrooms and portobello are good places to start. Separate the stems from the caps. You'll be using the stems for propagation, so you can enjoy the caps. Next, prepare your planting container. Any decent-sized tub will do—just make sure it's sterile. (If you're not sure, clean with bleach first and rinse thoroughly.) Put a layer of straw or shredded cardboard in the bottom, then moisten the soil and pack it down. Layer your mushroom ends on top. Follow this pattern with more layers of straw or cardboard and mushroom ends until the container is full. Cover the container with a lid or black plastic, making sure to poke holes in the top for air circulation. Store your container in a dark, cool room or garage, and make sure to keep the soil moist. In 2–4 weeks, you can harvest your very own mushroom crop.

## 63

### Embrace air layering to propagate large plants.

In the simplest terms, air layering is a technique that encourages living branches to develop roots. It's particularly useful for plants that are difficult to propagate, or for indoor plants that have lost their lower leaves and look bare and leggy. With a few simple tools you can learn air layering yourself.

### Materials:

- Sphagnum moss
- Twine or string
- Plastic wrap
- Electrical tape

### Instructions:

1. Wound the branch you want to take as a cutting. You can do this by gently peeling bark away from a small section of the branch (about 1") or cutting into a soft-stemmed plant and peeling the cut area back.

2. Take a handful of damp sphagnum moss and wrap it around the wound, then tie it in place with twine or string. If you don't have sphagnum moss handy, you can use potting soil, but you'll have to hold the potting soil in place with plastic wrap.

3. Wrap plastic wrap around the damp growing media to hold it tight against the branch, forming a pouch that holds the growing media in place.

4. Using electrical tape, secure the plastic wrap in place.

5. Wait and watch carefully. After some time (how long depends on the temperature and type of plant you're trying to air layer), you'll see roots pushing toward the edge of the plastic wrap.

6. Using sharp, sterile garden shears, cut the branch off below the newly rooted section.

7. Carefully remove the plastic wrap, but don't disturb the roots if possible.

8. Plant the newly rooted branch in fresh potting media. You'll probably need to stake it up at first, until the new roots become established in their new home.

## 64

## Set up your seedling lights on a timer.

Lots of gardeners start their vegetable gardens early by growing seedlings inside under artificial lights that are left on for 24 hours a day. This extra-long light cycle provides plenty of light for your seedlings to thrive and grow quickly. However, as you get closer to transplanting them outside, you need to gradually acclimate them to a more normal light cycle. Instead of trying to remember every day to turn off your lights, why not use an automatic light timer? These inexpensive devices are widely available and can take the stress out of trying to remember to turn the lights on and off.

## 65

# Plant a half pepper to easily grow pepper plants.

When it comes to peppers, Mother Nature has already crafted the perfect planting vehicle for pepper seeds: the pepper itself! This delicious package is designed to protect and feed seeds. Next time you're at the store, pick up an extra pepper (any type will do). When you get home, slice the pepper in half and bury it in regular seed-starting mix with the cut side up. Water gently and keep the soil warm. Many types of peppers have a long germination time, so it might take some time, but before long, you should have a pot full of pepper sprouts. Pick out the weakest sprouts and transplant the rest into separate containers.

## 66

# Try "tomato slice" propagation.

Like the plants they come from, tomato seeds are naturally tough. Surrounded by a protective gel, they are designed to withstand digestion and spreading by animals. This makes saving tomato seeds a little tricky—so why not skip that step and plant tomato slices instead? This simple trick is exactly what it sounds like: Cut thick slices of tomato and lay them on a bed of potting soil, then cover with about 1" of potting soil. Use slices from closer to the middle of the tomato to get the most seeds, and don't worry about doing anything to prepare the seeds. Keep the soil moist and warm—you should start seeing tomato seedlings within a week.

## 67

### Let fish emulsion fertilizer nourish seedlings.

Most seeds have everything an embryonic plant needs to survive, including enough food to get the plant started. But once your sprouts emerge and start to grow, you face a question: When do you start feeding your new plants? Feeding them with a strong fertilizer too early can kill them, but depriving them of any fertilizer means slower growth and less robust seedlings. One good option for seedlings is fish emulsion fertilizer. Widely available in garden centers, fish emulsion is gentle and contains a nice mix of macro- and micronutrients. Just beware: This stuff smells terrible, and your cats will love it, so make sure you store it in a sealed container and don't let your animals near your seedlings right after you water.

## 68

### Add side lighting to strengthen stretchy seedlings.

Starting your seeds early and indoors is the best way to stretch your growing season, but it's not without challenges. The biggest problem you'll face is likely to be a lack of light: Seedlings are light hungry, and too many gardeners have quickly discovered that a "sunny" windowsill isn't nearly bright enough to grow healthy seedlings. Seedlings that don't get enough light stretch and develop weak stems. If this sounds familiar, why not add some side lighting? You can use regular shop fluorescent lights, grow lights, or LED plant lights. This extra light may be just what your seedlings need to really thrive and stop stretching.

## 69

## Learn how to DIY graft to grow more robust, pest-resistant plants.

Grafting is another difficult-sounding technique that's actually much easier than it seems. It works particularly well on citrus—in areas where citrus grows, some gardeners create "fruit salad" trees that bear oranges, grapefruit, and lemons from the same tree! Grafting can also be used on most fruit trees to increase your stock cheaply. Follow these easy DIY steps to create your own grafted trees.

### Instructions:

1. You'll need a rootstock tree. It's best to buy a young plant as rootstock—and you'll want to get the same type of tree you're grafting. So, if you're grafting apples, for example, you'll want a young apple tree as rootstock.

2. Choose your "scion" plant. This is the term used for the plant you're grafting onto the rootstock. Take a piece of the scion that's approximately the same diameter as the rootstock.

3. Cut the top of the rootstock away, leaving a bare stem. Slice down into the rootstock with a very sharp knife. The cut should be about 1"–2" deep.

4. Trim the end of the scion into a wedge.

5. Drive the scion wedge down into the cut rootstock, ensuring as much direct contact between the rootstock and the scion as possible.

6. If you have grafting tape, wrap it snugly around the new graft. If you don't have grafting tape, you can use old pantyhose.

7. Plant your new tree and stake it up to protect the graft and hold it in place.

## 70

### Use air stones to help your cuttings root.

Rooting your cuttings in water is an easy, mess-free way to propagate plants—but it can be frustrating when your cuttings rot and never take root. One simple way to help them root faster is to drop a cheap aquarium air stone into your water container. Designed to provide plenty of oxygen for fish, air stones gently bubble the water and ensure your cuttings get plenty of oxygen. The trick for success is to use a relatively small stone—you're not trying to create a Jacuzzi for your cutting! Even a small increase in oxygen to the emerging root zone can result in more robust, healthier cuttings.

## 71

### Root your pothos vines in a glass of water.

Pothos vines, sometimes called devil's ivy, are some of the most popular houseplants because they're nearly indestructible. These tough and pretty vines can withstand poor light, uneven watering, lack of fertilizer, years between repotting, and even drafty rooms. With this in mind, it should be no surprise they're also some of the easiest plants to propagate. To turn your one pothos into many, cut off short pieces of vine. Take pieces with at least four sets of leaves. Trim off the lower two sets of leaves close to the stem and put the cutting in a glass of water with a few drops of fertilizer. You can keep the glass on a windowsill until new roots emerge from the cutting, changing the water every two weeks or so. When you see new roots, go ahead and pot your new vine.

## 72

### Turn your bathroom or kitchen windowsill into a propagation zone.

The single best advice you can get as a gardener is this: right plant, right place. When it comes to starting seedlings, this is doubly true. You want someplace warm and humid, with good light. And guess what—you might have a place exactly like this in your house already: a bathroom or kitchen windowsill. Unless you're planning on starting dozens of seedlings or cuttings, these sills are perfect places to get started. You might have to add some extra light, but you won't have to worry that your seedlings aren't getting enough warm, humid air.

# Chapter 2

# CONTAINER GARDENING

## 73

### Nest your containers for easy replanting.

Interiorscaping is the art of bringing nature inside and filling your living spaces with beautiful container plants—but there's no doubt it can be annoying when your plants start suffering inside and need to be repotted or rotated outside during the summer to perk up. Why not take a page from the pros and make life easy by nesting containers? This way, you can keep your decorative and beautiful container inside and never have to worry about repotting: Just set your houseplants still in their ugly black nursery containers straight into the larger container. For added ease, plug the bottom hole on the decorative container so you don't have to worry about water ruining your floors. When you need to switch plants, it's as easy as swapping out one interior container with another.

## 74

### Skip repotting your big plants—top-dress instead.

There's nothing quite as dramatic as keeping a large palm or ficus in a sunny foyer or by a big window—but as anyone who has tried to move a large container knows, these "statement plants" aren't easy to deal with, especially at repotting time. Here's a quick tip to get around the strain and mess of repotting your large plants: Top-dress them instead. This practice involves laying out newspapers or a tarp to catch any falling soil, then digging out the top few inches of potting soil and replacing it with new soil. When you top-dress, you can also use your trowel to break up the remaining soil so more air and water can penetrate the lower root zone.

## 75

### Use a funnel to target your fertilizer in heavily planted containers.

Fertilizer is the not-so-secret ingredient for healthy plants, but when it comes to fertilizing your bushy planters, you want your fertilizer to end up feeding the plants inside, not sliding off leaves and scattering everywhere. Make this job easier by saving an old kitchen funnel and putting it to work. When it comes time to fertilize, just poke the funnel down into the leaves and pour the recommended amount of fertilizer into the spout. This easy hack means you won't lose fertilizer and will be able to control exactly how much your plants are getting.

## 76

### Give your tropical plants a shower to mimic their natural habitats.

A good rule of thumb for growing any plant well is to mimic the conditions of its native area. For a lot of houseplants—think peace lily, philodendron, elephant's ear, ficus, dieffenbachia—this means the tropics. These plants thrive in warm, humid conditions with plenty of water and dappled light. Here's a tip that will give these plants a nice boost. Every so often, move them to your shower and give them a steam bath, then water them well and let them drain completely. The added jolt of humidity and warmth is just what they crave, and this will also help clean any dust and debris off their leaves.

# 77

## Plant in recycled culverts.

Take your vertical gardening to the next level with cool and economical containers made from corrugated steel culverts. You can either buy new culverts from plumbing supply stores, or, better yet, call your local city transportation department and ask if they have any extra culverts. You may need to cut the culvert to size before planting. This can be done with a circular saw with a metal blade—if this is daunting, ask for help, and always take safety precautions when working with electrical tools. To plant your culvert, dig into the soil a few inches to hold it secure, then stand the culvert upright and tamp down the soil. Partially fill it with gravel, cinder blocks, or old cans to save money and increase drainage, then fill the remaining space with potting soil mix, and plant!

## 78

## Repot directly in soil bags to avoid mess.

Instead of moving all that dirt by hand, you can make repotting easier by simply using the bag your potting soil came in as a planting container. This works best with a smaller container, usually smaller than 3 gallons. Simply cut the top off your bag of soil so it's completely open, then puncture the bag at least a dozen times. This will allow water to more easily flow through the bag so your plant gets better drainage. Now drop the bag into a pot and trim away extra plastic so the bag top is roughly at the soil level, then you can plant directly in the bag. When it comes time to repot the plant, you can just lift the bag out of the container whole so there's less mess.

## 79

## Use old sponges to increase water retention in containers.

Why spend money on water-retention crystals for your potted plants when you probably have "water-retention sponges" sitting around the house? This simple hack is a great way to increase water retention in containers and is easy and inexpensive. Just cut up a few old sponges and place them into the bottom of your container, or you can even throw them whole into the bottom of a container. The sponges will soak up liquid every time you water, so your plants will always have enough, and you can water less often.

## 80

## Save soil:
## Bulk up your containers with old bottles and cans.

Good potting soil is essential to healthy potted plants, but it's not exactly cheap. To save some money and stretch your soil further, try adding a layer of old cans or bottles to the bottom of larger containers. Not only will this add bulk so you'll need less soil; it also increases your container's drainage so water can't saturate the soil at the bottom of your pot. This will greatly reduce the risk of your plants suffering from root rot. Finally, using something bulky like cans or bottles also means your containers will be lighter and easier to move around and manage.

## 81

## Try planting in chimney-flue liners.

Tired of the same-old, same-old terra-cotta pots? Here's an inexpensive and interesting alternative: Use chimney-flue liners. These square terra-cotta containers are designed to protect the inside of your chimney flue from smoke and heat damage, but they also make really interesting planters. Mixing flue liners of different sizes and heights can create a visually dramatic container garden. If you're looking to create an interesting garden border, try lining them up to form a path. If your border is in a higher-traffic area where they might get bumped, bury the containers about 2" deep, then add gravel about one-third of the way up before filling with potting soil. This will make them more stable and harder to knock over.

## 82

### Make a watering can for your container plants from an old milk jug.

There's no reason to spend money on a dedicated watering can when you can easily make one at home. Old milk jugs work great, and it couldn't be any easier to turn them into watering cans. Make sure you save a jug with a cap and wash it very well—you don't want your watering can to smell like sour milk. Next, using a hole punch, skewer, or even a small drill bit, puncture the jug's cap with small holes (and decorate the jug if you're feeling artistic). Fill the jug with water—with or without liquid fertilizer, put the cap on, and you're ready to water your plants with a gentle rain.

## 83

### Stop soil leaking with coffee filters.

Container gardening means finding a balance between providing your plants everything they need to thrive and not destroying your house with errant dirt. This simple coffee filter hack makes it easier to nail that balance every time. When you're potting a new plant, add a coffee filter or two to the bottom of your container as a filter. The filter will still allow water to pass through, but it will stop soil from leaking out into your tray or onto the floor.

## 84

### Cut your pots when repotting orchids to protect your roots.

Orchids are notoriously fussy about being disturbed. In general, if you have a healthy orchid that blooms year after year, leave it alone for as long as possible. The unfortunate side effect of this plan for pot-grown orchids is roots that circle inside the container or roots that clamber outside the container and attach to the outside. Repotting a root-bound orchid means figuring out how to remove the container without damaging the fragile roots. Here's an easy trick: Break or cut away the original container. In most cases, you'll be able to cut away a plastic container or shatter a terra-cotta orchid pot without causing too much damage to the orchid roots. Once you've freed the plant, you can gently remove dead roots and repot. Don't worry if a few pieces of terra-cotta are still clinging to your orchid roots when you repot—they'll just join the potting soil!

## 85

# Boost your fertilizer game with slow-release pellets at repotting.

Healthy plants are fertilized plants, but it can be all too easy to forget to fertilize. While you can always spend some extra money to buy fortified potting soil, it's cheaper and just as easy to buy a bag of controlled-release fertilizer pellets and mix some into your potting soil. These pellets will provide about six months of continuous food. When the six months are up, scatter a few more tablespoons into the container, and you're good until it's time to repot next season. When looking for slow-release fertilizer, make sure to read the label—these products are different than typical granular fertilizer, which needs to be mixed with water. As always when using any garden chemical, follow the label's safety and dosing directions.

## 86

# Reduce overheating with white containers.

Are you lucky enough to have loads of direct light pouring into your indoor growing space? While that's better than not enough light, direct sunlight does have some issues of its own, including heating dark pots and potentially damaging small roots near the container walls or drying out your potting media. The solution here is simple: Use white or light-colored pots. These pots will reflect some of that intense heat instead of soaking it in. The result is cooler potting media and less frequent watering.

# 87

## Add a handful of perlite to your containers for better drainage.

Good drainage means healthy plants. This simple rule is true for almost every container plant, from desert-born cacti and succulents to the leafiest tropical houseplant. While most commercial potting mixes include nonorganic ingredients like perlite and vermiculite to increase drainage, these are usually the most expensive part of the mix, so the soil companies add only the bare minimum. (You can tell how much of this is in your soil by the concentration of little white pellets—the more, the better.) If you want to grow the healthiest plants possible, invest in a bag of your own perlite or vermiculite. At potting time, mix a few handfuls of perlite or vermiculite into your soil. When using these additives, read the label and always follow safety precautions to avoid breathing dust.

# 88

## Don't pack your containers with soil when you plant.

For most container plants—especially the tropical plants people love so much—it's more important to have aerated, loose soil that drains quickly and makes it easy for the plant's roots to get plenty of oxygen. Also, typical potting soil is made from peat moss, which breaks down relatively quickly and becomes compressed. So, instead of artificially starting this process, give your plants the gift of loose soil by wetting your potting media when you plant but not smooshing it down too hard in the container.

## 89

## Transform your old sinks and tubs into amazing planters.

Containers can be more than utilitarian objects that hold plants. They can double as garden features and design elements— and few large containers are as interesting and have as much potential as old tubs and sinks. Both of these interior fixtures come with drainage holes already created, so all you have to do to create your own unique container is lay some gravel in the bottom, then fill it with soil and plant. To help them blend in better with your landscape, plant your repurposed containers densely, then surround with complementary plants.

## 90

# Pay attention to the mature size when you plant in containers.

So, you're standing in front of a beautiful ficus plant in the garden center and thinking, "This would look great in my bathroom!" It probably would...at least for a while. But in reality, that adorable ficus is a monster in waiting—it wants to grow into a 100' tree with aerial roots and a spreading canopy. At some point, you'll either have to get rid of it or root prune it. The solution? When you're planning container gardens, look at the mature size of your plants before you buy them and make sure you have a plan for when that little sprout tries to turn into a forest giant.

## 91

# Make a small "standard" fruit tree to harvest container fruits.

Desperate to grow and harvest your own fruit but don't have the room for a full-sized fruit tree? No worries! With a little planning and ingenuity, you can grow dwarf fruit trees in containers and still harvest the fruit you crave. This technique works for everything from citrus to peaches and apples. Similar to stunting bonsai plants, the idea is to plant a young fruit tree in a fairly large container (at least 10 gallons). As the tree grows, aggressively prune its main trunk and side branches to create a dwarfed standard, or a tree with a single trunk that is still small enough to survive in the container.

## 92

# Collect your own worm castings for an easy, organic soil boost.

"Worm castings" is a nice way of saying "worm poop," but this stuff is garden gold. Created by earthworms as they munch on organic soil, worm castings add structure and drainage and are a great source of organic fertilizer. While you can buy worm castings, you can easily create a worm farm with minimal supplies. All you need is a 12"-deep bin with drainage holes, sand, newspaper or cardboard, compost, and worms. Start by adding a layer of sand to the bin, for drainage, then a thick layer of shredded paper (don't use glossy mailers—newspaper is recommended). Next add a layer of compost, then more shredded paper. Stir in the worms and feed them with the same kitchen waste you'd add to a compost bin. There shouldn't be any odor, so you can even keep a worm bin inside. When it comes time to "harvest" your black gold, sift the worms out to set up a new bin and use the leftover castings as soil additives.

## 93

### Add quick drama to a plain potted plant by adding cascading plants.

Looking to add a little flair to any potted plant? Why not add a cascading plant that spills over the side of the container? This is easy and can instantly elevate a simple container to a showstopper. Depending on your growing environment, good options for cascading plants include sweet potato vine, cascading snapdragon, lobelia, and many others. You can also use trailing succulents like string of pearls, string of nickels, and burro's tail for your drier indoor containers. When planting a cascading plant, position it near the edge of your container and be careful not to damage the roots of any other plants. For flowers and vines, it can help to soak the root ball before planting so it will get established faster.

## 94

### Use old spoons for working with small containers.

Working with small containers—especially if they're filled with spiny plants like cacti and some succulents—can be annoying and messy work. If you find yourself wishing for a tiny spade to work with small plants in small containers, look no further than your kitchen. Chances are you have some old spoons hanging around. Set these aside with your other garden tools and use them to help your container gardening. Spoons can be enormously helpful when it comes to adding soil, digging up and repotting small plants, and even distributing fertilizer.

## 95

## Plant a dugout garden in that fallen tree.

Creative containers don't have to cost a fortune—sometimes they can be as simple as what's literally lying around, including fallen tree trunks. If you have a large trunk, an ax or small chainsaw, and some brute muscle, consider hollowing out the log, then filling it with potting soil and turning it into a rustic and eye-catching flower bed. You don't have to hollow out the whole log; only remove enough wood for a decent depth of soil. A few inches can be enough to support flowers and vines. This is a lot of physical work, so be prepared with safety gear, including gloves and eye protection. The good news is that your new dugout garden will be virtually indestructible and last for many years.

## 96

# Turn your hanging container into a DIY flower ball.

Hanging flower baskets can be stunning additions to any porch or garden—and with minimal effort, you can level up your baskets by creating DIY "flower balls" that are bursting with flowers and trailing plants on the sides. Here's how.

## Materials:

- Wire hanging basket
- Coconut basket liner
- Shears or utility knife
- Container soil
- Slow-release fertilizer

## Instructions:

1. Line the basket with a standard coconut fiber or coconut coir liner, then plan your side-planting holes along the liner. Mark spots every 3" to show where the plants will go.

2. Cut X-shaped slits into the liner on the spots you marked.

3. Fill the basket liner with container soil up to the bottom of the X-shaped slits.

**4.** To plant the sides, gently remove the plants from the containers and plunge them one at a time into a bucket of water. Compress the root balls and soil with your hands, wringing out extra water.

**5.** Carefully insert the dripping root balls through the X-shaped slits from the outside.

**6.** Repeat until all the sides are planted.

**7.** Add more soil to the container.

**8.** Add a centerpiece plant, then line the sides of the basket with more bedding flowers.

**9.** Carefully add more container soil until the basket is full.

**10.** Toss in a few tablespoons of slow-release fertilizer pellets.

**11.** Before watering, lift the basket onto its final hook. If you water first, the basket may be too heavy to lift.

**12.** Water your flower ball and enjoy! The plants should quickly grow to create a vibrant flower ball.

**Tip:** Mix trailing vines into your side plantings for even more impact. With proper feeding and watering, your dwarf fruit tree will bear fruit just like its larger cousins.

## 97

# Add crushed eggshells to your container soil for free calcium supplements.

Calcium is necessary for all plants to grow, and some veggies will actually fail to grow without enough calcium. Next time you crack an egg, rinse the shell and throw it into a container to save it. When you have collected a small batch, crush the shells into small pieces and incorporate them into your container soil to provide a calcium boost. Similar to other types of calcium supplements like bonemeal, eggshells don't decompose quickly, so it's best if you can add eggshells to your container soil right at planting time or as early as possible.

## 98

# Cover outdoor container plants with old shower curtain liners during colder nights.

Container plants grown outside are more vulnerable to cold weather than in-ground plants for the simple reason that they don't have the insulation of the earth when temps drop. Exposed containers get cold, chilling the soil within. One of the best ways to protect your plants on cold nights is to water thoroughly before temps drop and then cover the containers with old shower curtain liners tented over the plants. This easy hack will protect your plants from cold wind and raise the humidity in the plants' environment. Just remember to remove the tarps the next morning before the plants are exposed to direct sun.

## 99

## Turn your coffee grounds into plant food.

Coffee isn't just popular with people...your plants also love a dose of the good stuff, via coffee grounds. Instead of throwing away coffee grounds, mix them into your potting soil or top-dress your containers with ½" of coffee grounds. While plants don't care about caffeine, they do appreciate the essential macro- and micronutrients that coffee grounds contain, including nitrogen, potassium, calcium, phosphorus, magnesium, iron, and more. Additionally, coffee grounds have a natural pH of about 6.7, which is perfect for most plants, so they can help keep your soil's acidity in the ideal range. If you have more coffee grounds than you can realistically use right away, you can also add the grounds to your compost pile.

## 100

## Add a layer of stones to containers to cut down on watering.

Landscapers have long known the value of stones. They discourage weeds, reduce soil erosion, and cut down on the amount of water lost to evaporation from the dirt. Next time you plant a container, consider adding a thick layer of stones or gravel to the surface of the soil—you'll get all the same benefits as landscapers do, plus the chance to make your containers more interesting with materials like marble chips, river stones, or even aquarium stones. Once you've added the stones, take care of the container as you normally would.

# 101

## Repot your orchids so they'll survive for the long term.

It's not immediately obvious, but most orchids for sale today are doomed to die, thanks to their containers. In their actual habitats, most orchids cling to trees or rocks. Their silvery or white roots act to absorb water and "breathe." When a grower wraps an orchid's roots in wet moss and then jams them into a plastic container, it's like slowly suffocating the plant. If you want your orchids to survive, give them plenty of air around their roots. This means repotting your orchids into a specialized orchid potting medium (you can buy this in most garden centers), using a container that drains freely, and displaying your orchid in a place that gets plenty of good airflow.

# 102

## Save money on soil with the upside-down container-within-a-container trick.

Potting soil is certainly more expensive than air, so here's a trick to save some money on potting soil for your large containers: Place a smaller container upside down inside the larger container before you fill it with potting soil. Ideally, choose a smaller container with lots of drainage holes to encourage drainage, or you can lay down a 1" layer of pebbles first so water can still seep out the bottom of your big container. This simple trick means you'll need a lot less soil to fill your larger container, plus your container will be lighter and easier to work with.

# 103

## Cut your phalaenopsis orchid spike (but leave room for reflowering).

Flowering phalaenopsis orchids are everywhere, but many people are confused about what to do with their declining flower spike. Here's the first thing: You'll need to snip off that dead flower spike. You can do this with a sharp, sterilized pair of shears or a knife, cutting close to the base of the leaves. If you want to encourage the plant to flower again from the same spike, try this trick recommended by the American Orchid Society. Instead of cutting at the base, cut the orchid spike higher up, leaving two of the formerly flowering nodes on the partial spike. This sometimes forces the plant to rebloom from the partial spike. This happens most often with single-branch flower spikes—plants with branching spikes are less likely to rebloom from an old spike.

## 104

# Line your container with a diaper for better water retention.

Here's an easy hack that will dramatically increase your container's water retention. Next time you're planting a container, bury a disposable diaper in the bottom. Modern diapers are so absorbent, they can easily hold 12 ounces or more of water, meaning you'll have to water much less. If you don't have room in your container for a full diaper, you can also shred or cut up a diaper and pile the pieces into the bottom, then add soil on top. The only caveat is to be aware of your container's extra watering-holding capacity—don't overwater and saturate your plant's roots.

## 105

# Stop root rot with a pot-within-a-pot technique.

When it comes to container gardening, thanks to root rot, it's just as easy to kill your plants by overwatering as by underwatering. Ideally, your containers should have fast-draining soil and never be left to sit in water. Here's a neat trick to achieve foolproof drainage while also making it easy to rotate plants and prevent mess—use an elevated pot within a pot. To make this work, first choose a larger decorative container, ideally one without any drainage holes in the bottom. Next, place gravel, stones, or even small bricks in the container, then rest your planted container on the elevation. When you water, the excess will run out and collect in the bottom of the larger container, where it will evaporate and increase humidity without risking root rot or damaging your floors.

# 106

## Create a water wick to keep your plants watered when you're gone.

Leaving your plants alone while you travel can be a nerve-racking experience, especially if you can't find someone you trust to water them while you're away. Here's a simple trick to put your mind at ease: Make your own self-watering system. All you'll need is a glass, jug, or empty 2-liter bottle and some paper towels or an old clean rag.

### Instructions:

1. Create a reservoir by filling the glass with water. You can add a little liquid fertilizer if you like.

2. Now make your wick. If you're using paper towels, twist several sections into a rope. If you're using a rag, ensure it's clean and free of any possible contaminants.

3. Insert the end of the wick into the reservoir. Make sure the wick goes all the way to the bottom of the reservoir. A dry wick can't move water!

4. Bury the other end of the wick an inch or two into your soil. Through the principle of osmosis, as the soil dries, it will pull water up from the reservoir through the wick.

**Tip:** You can use this same system to water more than one plant at a time. Just make sure your reservoir is large enough to hold adequate water, and create a separate wick for each plant.

## 107

# Convert your old wine bottles into water globes for container plants.

Water globes are a time-tested way to keep your plants watered if you can't do it yourself. The concept behind these devices is simple: A reservoir holds water that is allowed to seep into your soil as your plants need it. You can buy water globes, of course, but they're pricey. All you need to create an attractive water globe is an empty wine bottle and duct tape, plus a skewer or something sharp. Rinse the bottle out well, fill it with water, then tape the mouth of the bottle shut with a double layer of duct tape. Poke small holes in the tape "cap" so water can slowly seep out. Next, fasten this cap in place with a few quick wraps of duct tape. To use your globe, just insert it upside down into your container.

## 108

# Soak your plants before transplanting.

This is a great trick pros use when planting in containers: Plunge your plants into a bucket of water before transplanting. Giving your plants a quick dunk saturates the soil around the roots, so even if you're planting into dry soil, your new transplant will have plenty of water to help it get established. Soaking soil also helps break it up and free any pot-bound roots. If you want to give this a try, be prepared to make a mess—set up a bucket outside on the grass where it doesn't matter if you drop wet dirt and muddy water.

## 109

## Sprout potatoes in containers.

If you've ever accidentally sprouted potatoes in your pantry, you've seen how much these spuds want to grow. Next time that happens, why not plant them and get a steady supply of potatoes all season from your own garden? The easiest way to plant potatoes at home is in a container, such as a bucket or grow bag. It's best to start with sprouted potatoes (called seed potatoes). To plant, fill a container with about 5" of soil, then layer in your potatoes. Keep the soil slightly dry until foliage appears about two weeks later. As the potatoes grow, continue adding soil throughout the season. This will encourage more root growth, which means more potatoes. At the end of the season, dump the container out, and voilà! You'll have a season's worth of fresh potatoes.

## 110

## Repurpose aluminum cans as mini planters.

Aluminum cans are usually recycled or disposed of, but here's an interesting way to recycle them on your own. Instead of getting rid of them, start a kitschy or interesting collection of cans, then cut their tops off with a regular can opener. With a nail and hammer, add a drainage hole or two to the bottom of each can. You can use your new can planters for an interesting windowsill herb garden, or create a succulent collection with one succulent per can. Care for these unique planters is the same as for any container, but be careful not to knock them over when you water!

# 111

## Make your own fertilizer "tea" from compost.

This tip for making your own compost "tea" starts with only compost and water, but you can add anything from fish emulsion to seaweed to coffee grounds. To create your tea, cut an old T-shirt or piece of fabric into a 24" x 24" square. Pile up about 5 pounds of compost and other ingredients in the middle of the fabric, then tie it firmly shut with a string. Fill a bucket with rainwater or water you've let sit out for 24 hours, so the chlorine has evaporated. Submerge your giant "tea bag" in the water. Let it sit for five days, gently agitating the water once or twice a day. When the tea is a strong, dark color, remove the tea bag. Use the tea as a liquid fertilizer for container plants or young transplants.

# 112

## Put those old decorative colanders to work as planters.

These sturdy kitchen workhorses make really interesting hanging planters, and they can be easily painted with metal spray paint to complement your garden. To plant a hanging colander, use a coconut coir liner inside the colander. (You can cut these to fit if your colander isn't a standard size.) Once it's lined, treat it like any other hanging basket, filling it with container soil and then planting with your favorite flowers.

# 113

## Use broken terra-cotta containers for better drainage.

Terra-cotta pots are great for lots of reasons. Heavy enough to resist tipping over, these common orange pots are inexpensive, breathe better than plastic, and retain some moisture but also allow some evaporation to take place. They are, however, easy to break. But no worries! Why not start collecting your broken terra-cotta pieces and using them when you repot to increase drainage and reduce the amount of soil you need in larger containers. Just throw a handful of pot pieces into the bottom of a container when you plant. They can also be used as a potting medium for epiphytes like orchids—mix smaller broken pieces into your orchid container mix to stretch it further.

# 114

## Make your own glow-in-the-dark containers.

You can create a visually stunning night garden without a single light bulb or wire. Instead, all you need are some sturdy containers and a few cans of glow-in-the-dark paint or spray paint. Readily available online and in many big-box stores, today's glow-in-the-dark paint doesn't remotely resemble the weak glow-in-the-dark paint from previous years. This stuff seriously glows, and as the sun goes down after a sunny day, it will light up your painted containers with an incredibly dramatic display. Glow-in-the-dark paint works just like regular paint, so you can let your imagination go and mix colors or create interesting designs.

## 115

### Paint old tires in whimsical colors and plant in them.

Old tires are notoriously challenging to dispose of. They need to go through a special process to recycle because of the materials used in their creation. How about turning your old tires into planters instead? You can paint them with any colors you desire and use them to create fun and interesting little gardens. You can even stack or terrace your tires for a bit of three-dimensional interest (if you build them in a pyramid, you'll close off the holes in the middle of the tires). Your tire garden will survive year after year, needing only repainting when the colors fade.

## 116

### Keep your platters dry to avoid root rot.

Bad watering is probably the single greatest killer of container plants, whether that means not watering your plants enough or watering too much. In general, you'll need to water your containers evenly and frequently enough that the soil never dries out. But here's the trick: After you've watered, make sure you empty out any trays under your containers. When containers are allowed to sit in water, the bottom layer of soil becomes saturated and swampy. Few houseplants like growing in muck. When soil is too wet, their roots can't get enough oxygen, and bacteria can flourish. Over time, your plant may develop root rot and die. With one simple step—keeping the trays dry—you'll never have to worry about root rot.

## 117

### Create a lucky bamboo fish planter.

Lucky bamboo is one of the most popular houseplants in the United States because it's tough and can grow in almost any light conditions. Even better, this plant also thrives when growing in water with no soil! If you want to kick your lucky bamboo presentation up several notches, instead of using the standard vase as a container, try using a fishbowl with a live fish. Your plant and your fish will live in harmony: The plant's roots will add oxygen to the water, and the fish's waste will act as a fertilizer. Just remember to change the water frequently and strip off any leaves from the lucky bamboo that would be submerged, so they don't begin to rot and kill your fish.

## 118

# Make your own flower towers with PVC pipe.

A flower tower is a statement in your garden—and you can easily create your own with a large container and some large-diameter PVC pipe. You can find the pipe at most big-box stores or plumbing supply shops. To create your own flower tower, follow these steps.

## Materials:

- PVC pipe, at least 5" in diameter and cut to 6' length
- Tin can lid, about 4" in diameter
- Paper, markers, and scissors
- Power drill with 4" hole saw
- Large container
- Gravel
- Container soil

## Instructions:

1. Lay the pipe on the ground and mark your planting holes. Ideally, planting holes will be spaced about 4" apart vertically and staggered horizontally so you have maximum coverage of the pipe.

2. Using a can lid, trace a circle on a piece of paper, cut out the circle, then use this paper to trace the holes on the PVC where your plants will go.

3. Create the PVC holes using the 4" hole saw attached to a power drill. Always wear eye protection when working with power tools.

4. Stand the PVC pipe up in the container and carefully fill it with gravel from the top until the gravel is about level with the top of the container. This will help weigh the PVC down and hold it in place.

5. Fill in the container around the PVC with regular container soil.

6. To plant, select any bedding flower, herb, or trailing plant in 4" containers. Pour soil in from the top of the PVC tower until it fills to the bottom of the first hole.

7. Carefully slide your first plants into the tower, then add more soil from the top to hold them in place.

8. Repeat with layers of plants and soil until the soil reaches the top of the tower.

9. Add a top plant.

10. Plant more plants around the bottom of the tower in the main container.

11. To maintain your tower, you can water from the top, adding water and letting it soak in, then adding some more. Also make sure you're adding plenty of water to the base container—the tower will suck up water from the base, so you might find you need more water than you expect.

## 119

## Switch to coconut coir instead of potting soil to save space and money.

Most potting soils are a combination of composted peat and inorganic material like perlite or vermiculite. While this soil mixture is tried and true, peat deteriorates relatively quickly and becomes acidic. There are also environmental concerns about its use, because peat is a nonrenewable resource. If you're looking for inexpensive and renewable alternatives, consider coconut coir. This material is made from coconut husks, is pH neutral, has amazing water-holding capacity, and is easy to work with. Better yet, you can buy it in compressed blocks that store easily until you need them. For best results, throw in a few handfuls of perlite and some fertilizer.

## 120

## Salvage used tree pots to plant veggies that need a lot of soil.

There are lots of reasons you might want to grow veggies in containers—maybe you have a balcony or patio, or maybe you want to protect your crop from soilborne pests. For most vegetables, 1- and 3-gallon containers are fine, but robust vegetables like tomatoes need at least 10 gallons to grow well. Go to your local garden center and ask if they have any used black plastic containers you can have or purchase for a few bucks. These containers work perfectly for even big crops like corn, and you'll save a bundle.

## 121

# Save old bulbs from containers to plant outside.

Flowers growing from bulbs make popular gifts because they're beautiful and can provide flowers during the cold winter months, thanks to growers forcing flowering. A lot of growers recommend throwing away the bulbs when they're done flowering, but if you follow a few simple steps, you can save these bulbs for your own garden. Here's how to save bulbs from plants such as crocuses, daffodils, and snowdrops:

- Cut off the flower stalks when the flower is done, but leave the foliage intact.
- Move the plant to a cool and sunny windowsill. Continue watering and fertilizing.
- Depending on the time of year, your plant's foliage will eventually start to go dormant. This is normal! You can stop watering and fertilizing when the leaves start to turn brown.
- When the foliage is dead, trim off any remaining leaves and dig up the bulbs.
- Dry the bulbs in a cool, dry place.
- Store the bulbs in a cool, dry place. To prevent moisture, you can store them in sawdust, sand, or perlite.
- After the last hard frost, plant them outside in your garden!
- Note: If your bulbs were forced to bloom in the deep winter, it might take a year or two before they flower again.

# 122

## Sprout bulbs in style with a narrow-necked vase.

Instead of shelling out money for expensive winter flower displays, you can easily create your own bulb vases with a little planning. First, it's important to understand that most spring bulbs require a period of chilling, followed by warming temperatures. This signals to the bulb that it's time to start growing because spring has arrived. Second, because bulbs are self-contained, you can force them directly in water without any soil. With this in mind, here's how you can create your own winter bulb vases:

- Daffodils, crocuses, and tulips can all be forced at home, as long as you chill them first. To chill your bulbs, place them in a paper bag in the refrigerator. Daffodils and tulips need about three months, while crocuses need at least two months.

- Select narrow-necked glasses or vases for planting.

- Fill the container with water, then suspend the bulb in the neck of the container, making sure the bulb bottom is touching water.

- Place the bulb in a warm room, but not in direct sunlight, and add water as needed.

- New growth should emerge within weeks, followed by flowers.

## 123

### Learn how to root prune to keep your plants from taking over.

Root pruning only sounds complicated; in reality, it's a simple way to keep your plants a manageable size but still healthy. Root pruning is also used to give new life to pot-bound plants—plants whose roots have filled up their pot and have little room for soil. And it's simple! At repotting time, instead of moving your plant to a larger container, remove it from the container to expose the root ball. Using sharp snippers, trim away about one-third of the smaller roots on the outside of the root ball, along with any dead roots. Don't cut the thick main root (the taproot). When you're done, pot your plant back in the same container with fresh soil.

## 124

### Plant in raised outdoor containers to prevent bugs and increase drainage.

Adding large containers to your garden brings interest, color, elevation, and texture to your design—and it also means taking steps to protect the plants in those containers. Container plants need good drainage to thrive, which isn't really possible if a container is sitting directly on dirt. At the same time, anything in direct contact with the ground is an invitation for all sorts of pests to climb or even burrow up into. The solution? Elevate your containers off the soil level with a few bricks. Use decorative bricks if you want, or hide your bricks or stones with other plants. Either way, your container plants will appreciate it.

# 125

## Create a hanging herb garden with 2-liter bottles.

Growing fresh herbs offers so many benefits, but it can be hard to cultivate multiple plants in smaller spaces. This novel idea for a hanging herb garden created from empty 2-liter bottles makes it possible to grow herbs in front of almost any window, without risk of damaging your floors with water. It's not hard to create, but the key is careful watering: These 2-liter containers don't have any drainage, so you'll have to pay close attention to how wet the soil is.

### Materials:

- Empty and clean 2-liter bottles with caps (how many depends on your space)
- Scissors
- Skewer or hole punch
- Narrow-gauge wire
- Epoxy
- Hooks
- Container soil
- Herb plants

## Instructions:

1. Mark your cuts on the 2-liter bottles. These containers will be on their sides, so you'll be removing a section from the main body of the bottles about half the diameter of the bottle and 6" or so in length. Also mark small holes at the base and neck of the bottles for the wire to pass through.

2. Using scissors, cut away the middle section of the bottles. You can make the wire holes with a heated skewer or a hole punch.

3. Thread the wire through the holes, spacing the bottles about 12" apart along the length of wire and leaving several feet above the top bottle for hanging. The open sections of the bottles will all face up. Measure your bottle placements to make sure the bottles will be level.

4. Knot or crimp the wire at the bottom and secure it tightly against the bottom bottle.

5. Using epoxy, fasten the wire to the base and neck of each 2-liter bottle. Use enough to ensure a strong, watertight connection.

6. Fasten a hook to a secure place and hang the empty wire-and-bottle garden from your hook.

7. Fill the empty bottles with soil.

8. Plant your herbs and enjoy!

## 126

### Mix and match your containers to keep your garden visually interesting.

Whether you're growing your container plants outside in a formal landscape, or you keep a few potted plants on your windowsill, here's a tip to help create the most interest: Mix and match your containers. Think of the containers themselves as design elements and really stretch your imagination. Glass, metal, ceramic, plastic, and cement all make interesting choices, or use your imagination. Have an old teapot? Convert it into an ivy planter. Whatever you're using, if it doesn't have holes in the bottom for drainage, consider using the pot-within-a-pot technique so you can avoid overwatering (and switch plants easily).

## 127

### Water succulents with ice cubes to avoid overwatering.

Since succulents are mostly native to arid regions, overwatering them is the quickest way to kill them. Instead of guessing, here's a simple hack that will ensure they get a steady supply of not too much water: Use ice cubes. For a small succulent, tossing a few cubes of ice into the pot every week will ensure a slow trickle of moisture, with no fear that you're drowning your plants. For larger plants, you can use more ice. Not only will this keep your plants hydrated; you won't have to deal with messy overflows and trays full of water to empty.

## 128

### Soak your orchids in a sink full of water to keep them healthy.

Orchids are picky when it comes to being watered. Their thick white roots are designed to soak up drenching water like tissue paper, but they also need to completely dry out between waterings and like it when water can flow easily through and away from their containers, like rain. These conditions can be hard to meet inside, so here's a watering trick that makes it easier to thoroughly water your orchids without making a mess. Once a week, fill your kitchen sink partially with water (and perhaps add a few drops of liquid fertilizer) and soak your orchids for 10 minutes. When you're done, drain the sink and leave them in the sink to dry before moving them back.

## 129

### Add visual interest by planting in an old birdcage.

Birdcages offer a whimsical, Victorian-style touch to your garden. You can find decorative birdcages at consignment shops and flea markets. Before you plant your birdcage, you might want to give it a quick new coat of spray paint. To plant in the cage, either set containers directly in the bottom of the cage, or line the bottom with a standard coconut coir liner and fill with soil. Hang your birdcage from a hook on your porch or by your front door for an instant conversation piece.

# 130

## Make your own self-watering system.

Self-watering container systems like the EarthBox make it incredibly easy to grow vibrant herbs, vegetables, and flowers. While you can always opt to purchase the real thing, you can also make your own self-watering container with a few simple materials and a little elbow grease.

### Materials:

- Sturdy scissors for cutting the grate
- Plastic grate with small holes (same size or larger than the top rim of the tub)
- Large plastic bin
- 1½" PVC water-supply pipe, at least 4" taller than the tub
- Epoxy
- 4 pieces of 1" PVC pipe, each 3" long
- Power drill with a ⅝" bit
- Potting soil
- Gravel
- Granular fertilizer
- Black plastic sheeting
- Duct tape

### Instructions:

1. Start by measuring and cutting the plastic grate to fit snugly inside the bin, positioned so it hovers about 3" from the bottom of the bin. You may have to measure the bin interior 3" up from the bottom to get the right dimensions.

**2.** Using the water-supply pipe, trace a circle in one corner of the grate, then cut a hole in the grate for the pipe.

**3.** Cut a 3" square or circle from the opposite corner.

**4.** Using epoxy, glue the short pieces of PVC to the plastic grate. These will act as legs to hold the grate above the water reservoir.

**5.** Drill at least ten holes in the bottom 3" of the water-supply pipe.

## To Assemble and Plant:

**1.** Set the grate in the bin with the PVC legs underneath.

**2.** Pack the open corner with moist potting soil so the soil is level with the grate. This will act as a wick.

**3.** Slide the water-supply tube into the round hole across from the soil wick. It should stick up above the edge of the tub.

**4.** Spread a thin layer of gravel over the grate, leaving the soil wick uncovered.

**5.** Fill with potting soil. Add a few cups of granular fertilizer.

**6.** Cover the container with the black plastic and fasten in place with tape. Cut 6–8 X-shaped slits in the plastic, then plant your crops through these holes.

**7.** Fill the reservoir with water through the water-supply pipe.

**8.** To maintain the container, just make sure the reservoir has water.

# 131

## Boost your soil's water-holding capacity with crystals.

Some of the most popular container plants are water-hungry tropical plants that are sensitive to being underwatered. You can make life easier on yourself by adding water crystals to your potting soil at transplanting time. These crystals are designed to soak up and retain water, cutting down on the amount of water you have to add to the container. Water crystals are inexpensive and easy to find online or in most garden centers and big-box stores. Expect to spend about $10 for a bag that will last for many plantings. Using them is as easy as mixing a small handful into your container soil at potting time.

# 132

## Tuck some herbs into your containers.

If you're like a lot of cooks who garden, you're always looking for ways to get fresh herbs. Here's an easy trick that takes almost no extra effort: Scatter herb seeds in your existing containers. Picture a few vibrant basil plants alongside your Chinese money tree, or maybe some thyme trailing over the edge of your peace lily pot. Even if these plants don't have exactly the same care guidelines, the truth is that herbs are tougher than many people give them credit for—and the idea isn't to grow them to look at anyway! Hopefully, you'll be snipping at your herbs regularly for use in the kitchen.

## 133

### Design mixed containers in a professional way.

What's the difference between a professionally arranged container and a DIY one? In many cases, the only difference is the number of species you include in your container. If you want to create professional-quality containers, try mixing up the types of plants you include in your containers. Here are some quick pointers for elevating your container game:

- Put a taller accent plant in the middle of the container. Look for something that grows upright and doesn't spread.

- Use mixed flowers or herbs for the "bedding" plants, and don't space them out too far.

- Add one or two trailing plants for a cascading effect.

- When it comes to choosing which plants to use, a trip to your local garden center is a great idea, or you can look online for plants that grow well in your United States Department of Agriculture (USDA) zone.

# 134

## Inspect your new plants in the garden center before you buy them.

Few things are more disappointing than coming home from the garden center, excited about new plant purchases, and then discovering that your new plants are either root-bound or barely rooted at all. Here's a tip experts recommend to guarantee you're getting healthy plants: Pop the plants you want to buy out of the containers before you buy them, and check out the roots. You should see healthy white roots at the edge of a root ball. If you see roots circling the container or a mass of tangled roots with no soil, the plant is root-bound. If the roots are almost nonexistent and the soil ball crumbles in your hand, the plant isn't properly rooted yet. Set those down and keep looking for a healthy specimen!

# 135

## Don't neglect scent! Plant herbs, lavender, and other fragrant plants where people can smell them.

Gardens are fully sensory experiences. Plants aren't just pretty to look at—they involve all the senses. Smell is a very important sense, so don't neglect odor when you're thinking of potted plants. Make sure to pick a few plants that bring scent to your growing space. A favorite is putting a pot of lavender by your front door, so people might brush against it as they come in, releasing a wave of lavender perfume. Herbs like basil can brighten any room, and there are lots of flowering plants you can grow inside (like miniature gardenia) that have wonderful scents.

# 136

## Replant your overgrown orchids in their same old containers.

Orchids have never been more popular—you can likely pick up a gorgeous flowering phalaenopsis at the corner market for $10. If you can't bear throwing away such a beautiful plant when it's done flowering, sooner or later the question will come up: "How do I repot this thing?" Orchid roots aren't like other plant roots. They are covered in a silvery coating that soaks up water, and they often attach to the pot. Damaging or breaking these fragile roots can hurt your plant. Instead of prying your orchid from its old pot, you can simply plop the old pot right inside a new container filled with loose orchid mixture (which is not soil! It's a mix of bark, pellets, charcoal, and other big, chunky things with almost no water retention). The roots will soon travel into the new mixture, keeping your plant healthy and strong.

## 137
## Build your own strawberry tower.

There's nothing like garden-fresh strawberries, and no better way to get them than to grow your own. For many people with limited space, however, laying out a strawberry bed just isn't practical. Fortunately, there's something else to love about strawberries—they are excellent candidates for vertical gardening in towers. This simplified DIY strawberry tower relies on 5-gallon buckets instead of the traditional PVC piping. The advantage is that the plants won't become root-bound in a narrow pipe, so they'll be easier to water as the season goes on.

### Materials:

- 2 (5-gallon) buckets
- Power drill with 1½" or larger hole saw and ½" drill bit
- Potting soil
- Strawberry plants
- Gravel

### Instructions:

1. On each bucket, cut a dozen 1"–2½" planting holes in the sides, staggering the holes vertically and horizontally.

2. Flip each bucket upside down and drill another dozen holes in the bottom for drainage.

3. Fill a bucket with soil to the first row of holes.

4. Carefully insert the strawberry plant through the planting hole.

5. Add more soil and plants until the bucket is full.

6. Repeat with subsequent bucket.

7. Stack the buckets on top of each other to form a tower.

8. Cover the top bucket with a thick layer of gravel.

9. For the first week or so, keep your buckets in dappled light so the plants can recover from transplant shock. Move your plants to a sunny location and rotate the buckets every week so the plants get even sunlight. Water from the top, and you can also gently water from the sides in the gap between the rim of the bottom bucket and the top one.

## 138
### Try planting upside-down peppers.

Growing upside-down vegetables—including all kinds of peppers—offers a few powerful advantages, including saving tons of space, fewer pests and less fungal disease, and heavy yields if you do it right. To create your upside-down planter, you'll need a bucket, a hole saw, a coffee filter, and your soil and plants. Use the hole saw to cut a 1½" or 2" hole in the bottom of the bucket. Lay the coffee filter over the hole to prevent soil from escaping, then make a slit in the coffee filter. Insert the plant through the coffee filter so the plant is coming out the bottom of the bucket, and add soil to hold it in place. Fill the bucket with soil, mixing in granular fertilizer as you go. When you get to the top, plant a few herbs on top. Hang the bucket in a secure and sunny spot and water thoroughly.

# 139

## Make your own grow bags to hold vegetable plants.

Grow bags are a newer addition to vegetable gardening, and once you try them, you'll see why they've become so popular. They are light, are easy to store, and have excellent drainage. With a little preparation and some basic sewing skills, you can sew your own. All you need is the heaviest landscape fabric you can find and a heavy-duty sewing machine. First, cut a rectangle in the fabric that's twice as long as it is tall (12" x 24" will create a 1-gallon grow bag). To make your bag, fold the fabric the long way, then sew two open sides shut with durable thread. Leave one short side open for the top. Next, measure and stitch small triangular sections on the bottom to create the bag's bottom, then trim away the excess fabric. Turn your bag inside out, and voilà! It's ready to plant.

# 140

## Add lettuce to your hanging baskets to grow greens effectively.

This simple hack takes advantage of your existing hanging baskets to provide a source of leafy greens like lettuces. All you need to do is tuck a few lettuce plants along the edges of your regular baskets, then provide regular and plentiful moisture. The other plants in the basket will protect the leafy greens from harsh, direct sunlight, and you'll be able to harvest greens as you need them, planting new ones when you run out. Better yet, because you're using hanging baskets, your greens won't attract as many pests. You can do this with any leafy green, including red and green lettuces and Bibb lettuce.

# 141

## Boost the calcium content of soil in tomato containers with powdered milk.

One of the great frustrations for tomato growers is a condition called blossom-end rot. This disease, which causes watery, black rot on the tomato fruit, is caused by a lack of calcium. By the time you see blossom-end rot, it's too late to treat it—the best you can hope for is to prevent it in future tomatoes. Here's a trick old-timers use to make sure their tomatoes get plenty of calcium: Add ½ cup of powdered milk when you plant your tomato containers. Milk is full of calcium, and it's in an easily accessible form in powdered milk.

# 142

## Make a floating garden that never needs watering.

This DIY project was inspired by the genius gardeners at Orlando's Walt Disney World, who create floating gardens that dot the park's many lakes. These incredible flowerpots are easy to make and can be floated in any fresh water, from a decorative fountain to a backyard pond.

### Materials:

- Polystyrene foam circle, 2" thick
- 3 narrow pool noodles for the sides
- Latex glue (or any glue that works on Styrofoam)
- Latex or Styrofoam-compatible, waterproof black paint
- Power drill
- Capillary mat or felt
- Utility knife
- Potting soil
- Bedding plants

## Instructions:

1. Cut the polystyrene into a circle the diameter of your final garden. Include the width of the pool noodles; they will form the sides of the planters.

2. Cut and form the first pool noodle into a circle and glue to the polystyrene circle.

3. Stack the second and third noodles on top of the first, building the sides of your planter.

4. Paint the entire planter, inside and out, with the waterproof paint. Two or three coats may be necessary. Let the paint dry and harden.

5. Drill 4"–6½" holes through the bottom pool noodle at even intervals. This will allow excess water to drain away.

6. Line the bottom of the planter with capillary mat or felt.

7. Cut a 1" hole through the bottom of the planter.

8. Cut a wick from the capillary mat or felt and thread through the bottom hole. It should hang at least 12" below the planter into the water.

9. Plant with potting soil and bedding plants.

10. Float the container!

# 143

## Create a rustic and retro display with mounted tin can planters.

Most people don't think of "rustic" when they think of vertical gardening, but maybe that's because they've never seen a vertical tin can garden. This inexpensive DIY approach turns your old tin cans into hanging planters, perfect for anything from herbs to greens to houseplants. Best of all, you can knock this together with supplies you probably have around the house, plus some plants. You can use an existing wall, or you can recycle an old pallet or use a sheet of plywood. Simply nail or screw tin cans to the wall, spacing them however you'd like. Instead of planting in them directly (although you certainly can!), it's easier and cleaner to add a 1" layer of gravel for drainage, then drop potted plants into the cans.

# Chapter 3

# OUTDOOR GARDENING

## 144

### Use old cardboard boxes to suppress weeds.

Even the most dedicated gardeners often don't enjoy the back-breaking work of weeding to keep their beds clean. This clever idea uses common cardboard boxes to suppress weeds and act as mulch. Instead of putting your old cardboard boxes in your recycling bin, flatten them and save them for spring. When you're ready to plant, lay the cardboard on the bare dirt, either leaving your rows open or cutting holes in the cardboard where you want to plant. A thick layer of mulch over the cardboard will hide it, while underneath, the thick cardboard will prevent weeds and help your soil preserve moisture.

## 145

### Include bee-friendly plants in your garden for pollination.

Bees are essential for any ecosystem where they live. These prodigious pollinators ensure the survival of countless species of flowers and plants (and their honey is pretty delicious). With bee populations under strain from a strange disease that causes massive die-offs, gardeners should all do their part by planting bee-friendly flowers to attract and encourage bees. If you're not sure what flowers bees in your area like, call your local agriculture extension office. They should be able to help recommend bee-friendly plants.

## 146

## Know your USDA zone (and what that means) to set yourself up for gardening success.

When it comes to planning your garden, the two most important factors to keep in mind are the amount of rainfall you receive and the average low temperatures during the winter. Fortunately, the United States Department of Agriculture (USDA) makes it easy to track your winter temps. The USDA zone chart divides the country in thirteen zones, with one being the coldest and thirteen being the warmest. Consult this chart when you're planning your garden to make sure you're planting things that will thrive in your area. Find it here: https://planthardiness.ars.usda.gov.

## 147

## Mow your yard in a spiral so you don't have to lift your mower.

Mowing is hard work, especially if you're using a push mower—even if it's an automatic. At the end of every row, you still have to push down on the mower and swing it around to start the next row. Here's a cool trick that not only makes your job almost effortless; it also creates an eye-catching pattern in your grass: Mow in a spiral. Just start in the center of your yard and mow in increasingly larger circles until you get to the borders. The result is less backbreaking work and a spiral-cut yard your neighbors will envy.

# 148

## Build a terraced planter from fence posts to maximize growing space.

Not all of us have the luxury of space, but that shouldn't stop you from growing great veggies or strawberries. This DIY terraced garden can be quickly assembled in an afternoon with some basic tools and will dramatically increase the square-foot potential of your garden space.

### Materials:

- Fence posts or 4' x 4' boards
- Landscape fabric
- 6" screws
- Power drill
- Garden soil

### Instructions:

1. Begin by drawing your garden. You want at least 6" of planting room on each terrace level, so if the bottom layer is 4' x 4', the second terrace should be no more than 3½' x 3½'. At this size, you can create four terraces of the following sizes: 4' x 4', 3½' x 3½', 3' x 3', and a top layer of 2½' x 2½'.

2. Cut the fence posts for the different steps. You'll need four sides for each layer.

3. Clear your space and lay landscape fabric under the bottom terrace.

4. Create your first step by laying the cut fence posts on the ground. Use two 6" screws on each corner to drill the structure together.

5. Fill the bottom layer with garden soil and tamp it down, then water it so the soil settles. You want the dirt level with the top of the bed side.

6. Build the next layer and fill with soil, then tamp and water.

7. Repeat with subsequent layers.

8. Plant the perimeter of each layer and the top with vegetables such as peppers, lettuce, herbs, or other non-vining crops.

## 149

# Make DIY suet cakes to feed birds in the winter.

Suet is fat that is often used to create bird food. Suet feeders are especially helpful in the winter, when birds have a harder time finding energy-dense food. You can buy suet feeders for birds, but they're so easy to make at home that there's no reason to spend the extra money. To make your own suet feeder, mix 2 cups of warm liquid fat (beef, pork, or lard will all work) with 2 cups of cornmeal and 1 cup of peanut butter. If you're feeling generous, add birdseed, chopped nuts, dried fruit, honey, or sunflower seeds. Pour this mixture into an empty tuna can or any type of mold, then freeze it until it's solid. You can hang the suet cakes in mesh or wire bags from trees in your yard, then wait for your feathered guests to arrive.

## 150

# Water your grass less often but more deeply.

A healthy yard needs regular water, but with water restrictions and high water bills, it's important to conserve water. Fortunately, you can have both: less water use and an emerald-green yard. The trick isn't to water your yard more often but to water it more deeply. You'll quickly discover that you won't need to water as often if you're giving your yard plenty of water when you do turn on the sprinklers. Most yard grasses need at least 1" of water a week. To measure how much you're watering, put a glass in your yard and turn on the sprinklers. Time how long it takes to get 1" of water in the glass. This is how long you should be running your sprinklers...but only once a week.

## 151

### Use a posthole digger to quickly plant flowers or veggies.

Here's a trick to get those bedding flowers or vegetable transplants into the ground without ruining your knees or spending all day crouched over the dirt. All you need is a simple manual posthole digger, the kind used to dig holes for posts and mailboxes. These devices can be used in a standing position and make it easy to dig a shallow, wide hole perfect for most transplants. Once you've dug the holes, you can go back and plant everything, then cover with soil. If you have a really large garden, consider renting an electric posthole digger to make the job even easier.

## 152

### Check your soil's pH level with vinegar and baking soda.

Soil pH is a measure of how acidic or alkaline your soil is. The pH meter has measurements from 0–14. A reading of 7 is neutral. Anything below that indicates your soil is acidic, while anything above 7 means your soil is alkaline. Most vegetables like a slightly acidic soil, with a reading of 6–7 pH. This simple hack helps you figure out if your soil is acidic or alkaline. To begin, collect two soil samples, each measuring 1 cup. Add ½ cup of vinegar to one sample. For the second, mix the soil with 1 cup of distilled water, then add ½ cup of baking soda. If the vinegar sample fizzes, your soil is slightly alkaline. If the baking soda sample fizzes, your soil is mildly acidic. If neither sample fizzes, your soil is neutral.

# 153

## Target fertilizer distribution in thick beds using PVC pipe.

While fertilizer is essential for healthy plants, it can get pricey. If you're dealing with heavily planted beds or large shrubs, you want to make sure your fertilizer is actually getting to the root zone of the plants you want to feed. This trick with a regular PVC pipe makes it simple to direct fertilizer exactly where you want it, even while you're standing comfortably outside the bed. All you need is a length of ½" or ¾" PVC long enough to reach into your bed, plus a small funnel. While standing outside the garden, position the PVC at the base of the plant you want to feed and funnel granular or controlled-released fertilizer through the pipe.

# 154

## Deadhead your flowers to get more blooms.

Flower gardeners prize long-lasting displays of color, and dead-heading is one way they get them. Deadheading is the practice of removing dead or dying flowers from plants. It works because even dying flowers still require energy from the plant, meaning the plant has less energy for new flowers. So next time you see flowers starting to turn brown and die, snip them off right away. This trick also works for orchids like vandas (but isn't recommended for phalaenopsis). After the first three flowers have dropped from a spike, remove the whole spike. The plant will recover faster and bloom earlier. You can save the cut flowers for an inside display.

# 155

## Make a quick tomato trellis from string.

There are two types of tomatoes: indeterminate, which grow more like vines and need to be staked up, and determinate, which grow more like shrubs and don't need staking. There are lots of ways to stake up indeterminate tomatoes, but here's a trick the pros use to hold costs down. Instead of building something elaborate, train your tomatoes to grow up a wire or string hanging from a frame made of boards or pipes. The key is to aggressively train your tomatoes so there's only one main growing stem. This means pinching off any suckers or side branches and tying the main branch to the string. When it reaches a comfortable height, nip off the top growing point. The other advantage? You'll get bigger tomatoes.

## 156

### Mark your beds using flour.

If you've ever designed a garden bed, you've probably come across this standard advice to lay out the beds: Use a rope or garden hose. This works, but it means you must have a spare hose or rope and don't mind lugging it around. Why not make it easier on yourself and instead use all-purpose flour? A thick line of flour on the ground is easy to see and, if you change your mind, even easier to rub into the dirt and try something else. Better yet, you don't have to clean it up. Flour is totally organic and will wash into the dirt at the first contact with water.

## 157

### Create perfectly straight edges using boards.

Gardening isn't usually thought of as precise work, but sometimes nothing but a really straight line will do, especially when it comes to edging. If you need to create a really straight line, try using a board to help guide your shovel. Simply laying a straight board on the ground and using it as a guide for your shovel means you won't stray from your desired line, and you'll get a perfectly straight edge when you're done. The board also makes the actual edging easier, since you can lever your shovel against the wood to pry up shovelfuls of soil.

## 158

## Use shade-cloth covers for lettuces and other tender veggies.

Shade cloth is a specially designed landscape material that's used to reduce the amount of direct sunlight plants get. It's regularly used in sunny areas to protect plants like orchids and young nursery plants that don't like full sunlight. You can import this same technique into your garden, especially early in the season when your plants are still young and might appreciate the added protection. You don't have to buy expensive shade cloth—you can use leftover landscape fabric in a pinch, or even a roll of screening material.

## 159

## Use buckets to carry mulch and save your back.

Gardening is great exercise, but who doesn't appreciate a hack that makes moving mulch less backbreaking? Employing this simple idea can help you transport and spread mulch more easily, with less mess and less lifting. Instead of loading up your wheelbarrow with a pile of mulch, then dumping it on the ground and spreading it with a rake, try putting the mulch into smaller buckets and loading them into your wheelbarrow. After wheeling the buckets of mulch to the bed, it's relatively easy to pick up a smaller bucket of mulch and pour it directly where you want it to go. Your back will appreciate less lifting and less raking, and there's less cleanup when you're done.

# 160

## Create a hanging tomato garden with 5-gallon buckets.

Healthy tomatoes are vigorous, fast-growing plants that can thrive in surprising conditions—including growing upside down. This method of growing tomatoes from hanging bags or buckets was popularized by the Topsy Turvy growing system, but you can also create your own upside-down planters at less cost. Because heavy fruit can break the vines, consider planting cherry tomatoes or mid-sized tomatoes.

### Materials:

- 5-gallon bucket
- Sharp utility knife or power drill with hole saw
- Screen (window)
- Electrical tape
- Tomato plant
- Chain or rope to hang the bucket
- Potting soil and fertilizer

### Instructions:

1. Cut a 2"-wide hole in the bottom of the bucket, using either a sharp utility knife or a hole saw on a power drill.
2. Drill or cut two ½" holes in the bottom for additional drainage.

3. Flip the bucket right-side up and cut a piece of window screen to fit the bottom of the bucket. Tape it in place with electrical tape to hold it in position.

4. Cut an X in the screen through the larger hole in the bucket.

5. Prepare your tomato for planting by removing the bottom few sets of leaves.

6. If it's possible to reach the top of your bucket when hung, use the chain or rope to hang it in its final place. Hanging it now means you won't have to lift it later—a full bucket is heavy!

7. Insert the tomato, including the newly stripped part of the stem, through the hole in the bottom. Hold the tomato in place with one hand while adding enough potting soil to the top of the bucket to support the tomato.

8. Carefully add the rest of the potting soil, filling the bucket close to the rim.

9. Add a handful of fertilizer to the top.

10. Hang the bucket if it's not already hung up. (WARNING: As your tomato grows, the bucket will get even heavier. Make sure it's hung from a sturdy place to prevent damage or possible injury.) Water the bucket until water seeps from the drainage holes.

11. To care for your tomatoes, keep the soil evenly moist but not soggy. Place the hanging tomato in a sunny spot where it can get at least 5 hours of direct sunlight each day.

## 161

### Leave grass clippings on the yard as fertilizer.

The pursuit of the perfect grassy yard can be time-consuming and expensive—so take some of the work and cost out by simply leaving grass clippings on your yard. For grass that is regularly maintained, leaving grass clippings behind instead of bagging them up and carting them away makes good sense. The clippings are rich in nitrogen and act like a natural compost or fertilizer as they decompose. They also release water and help the soil retain moisture. The key to using your clippings, however, is not to let the grass go too long between cuttings. Long cuttings may pile up and actually kill the grass underneath.

## 162

### Recycle wine corks into plant labels.

This simple hack isn't just practical and free; it also looks really sophisticated and unique. Instead of tossing your old corks from wine bottles, try converting them into funky plant tags. All you need is wine corks, a permanent marker, and some bamboo skewers. Write the plant name on the cork, then stick the cork on a 12" skewer. The corks are weather resistant, so you can stick your new label in the ground in your garden or in containers. When your seedlings emerge, you won't have to remember what you planted where!

## 163

### Create living edging with cinder block.

Cinder block may not be the first thing that comes to mind when you think about garden hardscaping, but it's an inexpensive and surprisingly versatile material. To create a living edging on your beds, line up cinder blocks end to end with their holes facing up, then fill the holes with soil, and plant. You can add flowers, herbs, or even small vegetables. To make the edge more decorative, paint the cinder blocks before placing. Once your cinder block edging is in place, it will be impervious to weather and need no maintenance over time, plus you can replant it every year with different plants.

## 164

### Train your vines using zip ties.

Vines of all types are known for their fast, vigorous growth. In fact, if you don't take steps to control vines, they can easily overrun a trellis or fence. If you are looking for a way to control your vines, try using standard zip ties. These inexpensive, sturdy plastic ties are widely available and won't deteriorate in weather. They are also strong enough to hold up even the thickest vines (you can make chains of zip ties for very large vines). If you're growing tomatoes, you can also use zip ties to quickly and easily tie your indeterminate tomatoes to the support without messing around trying to tie intricate knots in twine or string.

# 165

## Build a quick DIY raised bed from cinder block.

Here's another use for cinder block: Create an instant raised bed with no tools. Just outline your raised bed on the ground, lay down your landscape fabric, and then use cinder block for the walls. A single course of cinder block will create a raised bed 8" tall, which is high enough for many smaller vegetables. If you want a deeper raised bed, use two layers of cinder block to create a 16"-tall border. Once the blocks are in place, you can paint them as desired so they complement the rest of your garden. A cinder block raised bed will last for years with little or no maintenance.

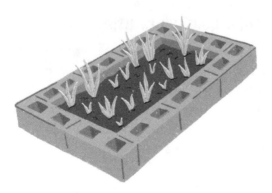

# 166

## Use old pantyhose to fasten epiphytes or orchids to your supports.

Epiphytes are plants that grow on other plants. Good examples of epiphytes include some types of ferns, orchids, and bromeliads. If you live in a warmer place where epiphytes can be grown outside, mounting these in trees can result in truly breathtaking landscapes—but simply tying them into trees can damage the tree if the string or rope girdles the branch. Instead, save up some old pantyhose (or buy new inexpensive ones) and use them as plant ties. The fabric will stretch as the tree grows and might even blend in with the tree bark. Also, because the material is porous, it will allow air and water to reach your plant without raising the risk of rot.

# 167

## Plan your garden using the mature size of trees and shrubs.

Overplanting is tempting. After all, you want your new garden to look lush from the day you plant it. Unfortunately, though, this leads to a common mistake in garden planning: the overstuffed garden. Next time you're considering adding a plant to your landscape, look at the mature size of the plant before you plant it. Just because a shrub or sapling is in a 3-gallon container in the garden center doesn't mean it won't grow into a towering tree. A little planning ahead in the beginning can save you money and effort later on.

## 168

### Take advantage of free garden planning apps and websites.

Beautiful gardens often begin on paper. Planning a landscape or even a vegetable garden is an indispensable step when it comes to using your space, but it can be a time-consuming process if you use pencil and paper. The good news is that there are plenty of time-saving and free digital landscape-planning tools, such as *Garden Planner* and *Smart Gardener*. Depending on which app or website you work with, these programs allow you to create a virtual 2D image of your garden and see how it would look with a variety of hardscape features and plants. They're also easy to use, and many offer excellent functionality with no charge.

## 169

### Water in the early morning to conserve water.

Tired of high watering bills or the feeling that much of your effort is wasted because the water just evaporates? Try switching to watering early in the morning. Watering earlier, before the heat of the day really kicks in, means you'll lose less moisture to evaporation as your soil soaks up the moisture. Your plants will also benefit from being fully hydrated before the sun bears down on them. Additionally, watering in the morning gives all that extra water sitting on your plants' leaves time to evaporate, which decreases the risk of fungal infections and other diseases.

## 170

# Create an eco-friendly and money-saving DIY rain barrel.

Collecting rain not only saves money, but also provides your plants with chemical-free water. While there are lots of premade rain barrels for sale, you can make one yourself in an afternoon.

## Materials:

- Large outdoor plastic garbage can with lid
- Water spigot with washers
- Watertight adhesive caulk
- Flexible downspout
- Power drill

## Instructions:

1. Cut a hole on the side of the can, down near the bottom, and install the spigot. Put washers both inside and outside the can and seal the spigot with adhesive caulk to hold it in place and ensure it doesn't leak.

2. Next, cut a hole in the lid just big enough for the downspout, then drill two ½" holes near the top 1" of the can to protect against overflows.

3. Hook the downspout up to your gutter and insert it into the lid, then attach a hose to the downspout.

4. Next time it rains, you can begin to nourish your plants with rainwater.

## 171

### Pinch off tomato suckers to train your vines.

Because tomatoes themselves are so fragile, it's tempting to think tomato plants are also tender. Nothing could be further from the truth. Indeterminate tomatoes, or those that grow like vines, are fast-growing, hungry, and vigorous plants. As the season wears on, controlling these plants can become a serious chore, as they try to overgrow any support you create for them. To make things easier, take a tip from the pros and aggressively prune your tomatoes. This means removing all the "sucker" shoots (side shoots that emerge between the main stem and the side branches) as well as trimming the tops from your tomato plants so they don't get too tall.

## 172

### Convert your tiki torches into LED light clusters.

This modern spin on tiki torches converts your old tiki torch into a long-lasting light feature in a few minutes. If you have old tiki torches in your shed or garage that are out of fuel, all you need to complete the conversion to LED lights is one small Mason jar and a cluster of LED lights for every tiki torch. Fill the jar with the lights, leaving the battery pack and switch free so you can easily reach it. Remove the old fuel container from the tiki torch, but save the black top. Set the jar inside the open torch and replace the black top. At night, turn the LED lights on—the bright lights will bleed through the wicker tiki torch, creating a spectral and beautiful light display.

## 173

### Remove immature fruit to grow giant specimens.

If you've ever seen pictures of monster vegetables and wondered, "How does a vegetable get that big?" then this hack is for you. One way to get bigger fruit is to remove some (or most) of the blossoms from your fruit or vegetable plant. This will encourage the plant to put extra energy into the fewer remaining fruits, resulting in bigger fruit. While the plant is growing, make sure to provide plenty of fertilizer as well.

## 174

### Create an easy vertical garden outside to grow more in small spaces.

For gardeners with small growing spaces, the trick to finding more space isn't to go out...it's to go up. Vertical gardening is a time-tested method to grow crops like lettuce, herbs, peppers, and strawberries in a small space, while also getting added protection from insects and disease. There's no reason to spend a lot of money buying a vertical garden kit or stackable containers when you can easily create your own vertical garden with any rack or shelving system. In a pinch, you can even mount containers to existing structures like walls. The most important thing to think about with your vertical garden is sun exposure—make sure your plants are getting plenty of direct sunlight.

## 175

# Attract hummingbirds with a DIY hummingbird feeder.

Hummingbirds are welcome visitors to any garden because they're beautiful and help pollinate plants—and better yet, they're not terribly difficult to attract. This homemade hummingbird feeder isn't as pretty as some of the more expensive versions for sale, but it's easy to build and will attract hummingbirds to your yard.

## Materials:

- Plastic bottle with top
- 1¼-cup Tupperware container with red lid
- Utility knife or scissors to cut the bottle
- Hot wire or drill bit
- Hummingbird food
- String to hang the feeder

## Instructions:

1. Use the plastic bottle top to trace a circle in the center of the Tupperware lid.

2. Cut a hole in the Tupperware lid large enough so you can insert the upside-down bottle with the cap on into it. Insert the bottle upside down into the hole to test its fit. It should be snug enough that the bottle cap is firmly gripped by the Tupperware lid.

3. Punch four holes in the Tupperware lid near the four corners. Each hole should be a little under ¼" wide and far enough from the edge that the hummingbirds will still have a place to stand while they feed.

4. Using a hot wire or drill bit, create a hole in the bottle cap. This hole should be no more than ½" wide so the feeder won't overflow.

5. Unscrew the bottle from its top and fill the bottle with hummingbird food. With the bottle upright, screw the top back on.

6. Invert the bottle so the Tupperware fills up with hummingbird food. The birds should be able to easily reach the food through the holes in the Tupperware lid.

7. Tie the string around the bottle and form a loop as a hanger.

8. Hang in your garden!

## 176

# Add shallow water features to attract butterflies.

Butterflies are more than just pretty visitors to your garden—they are also pollinators that help trees and flowers reproduce. Many garden experts recommend planting butterfly-friendly plants to bring in these winged visitors, but it's also a good idea to provide an appropriate water source for them. Most butterflies don't actually drink water—they get their liquid from nectar—but water is still vital for a behavior called "puddling." This occurs when butterflies gather around a shallow water source so they can soak up minerals and other nutrients from the mud or rotting organic matter around the water. To create your butterfly puddling station, begin with a shallow basin, like a birdbath, and add a layer of sand to the bottom. Next, add a few larger stones, then fill up the basin with water so the stones are partially submerged.

## 177

### Supplement your plants with Epsom salts for a boost of magnesium.

Avid tomato growers have been juicing their plants with Epsom salts for years, because they provide a healthy dose of magnesium as well as additional micronutrients, and they help balance your soil's pH. If you want to experiment with this inexpensive and common plant supplement, you have a few options. You can mix 2 tablespoons per gallon of water and apply as a spray, or you can add ½ cup per mature plant directly to the soil when you plant. You can also scatter Epsom salts directly on the soil right before watering. Just remember to always use pure Epsom salts, avoiding any product with added fragrance or coloring.

## 178

### Mulch, mulch, mulch to save money and grow better plants.

Mulching your garden is one of the easiest ways to save time and money and keep your plants thriving. A thick layer of mulch helps keep moisture locked into the soil while suppressing weeds, and as it decomposes, it also enriches your soil. The only downside to mulching can be its expense: If you have to rely on bagged mulch for even a medium-sized garden, you could end up spending a lot. Instead, try making your own mulch. You can mulch leaves and yard waste by piling the debris up and running your lawn mower over it. For larger branches, you may have to rent a wood chipper.

## 179

## Create DIY molded concrete containers.

You'll never look at concrete the same way again after you've mastered making your own molded concrete containers. This simple hack is limited only by your imagination—all you need is concrete, an exterior mold, and an inner mold to create the open space in your container. Begin by mixing the concrete. Prepare your outer mold by spraying it with oil (this will make it easier to release the container). You can make molds out of any shape you like, including plastic jugs, fabric bags, and even other garden containers. Fill your interior mold with an inch or so of concrete, then set your inner mold in the center. Continue filling around the edges with concrete until the concrete is level with your exterior mold. Shake the molds as you go to eliminate air bubbles and settle the concrete. Once it's full, let it dry for 12 hours, then remove the inner mold first, followed by the outer mold. Let the concrete cure for several days before painting and planting.

# 180

## Call before you dig, for safety's sake!

Always check with your utility company before digging on your property, especially if you're using any type of power tool. In more densely populated areas, you might be surprised to find out how many buried hazards are in your yard. This can include old gas lines, electrical lines, plumbing, septic drain fields, sprinkler lines, and more. In some cases, hitting a buried line with a shovel is just a minor inconvenience. In other cases—like if you hit a major electrical line—it can be deadly. So before you dig, always make sure to call your local utility company and double-check that there are no nasty surprises waiting for you underground.

# 181

## Use DIY bags to support and protect vertical melons.

Homegrown melons put store-bought melons to shame—so it's a pity many gardeners avoid growing them. These vigorous vines require a lot of space, which many gardeners don't have. The solution is to grow melons vertically on a sturdy trellis and use slings to support the suspended fruits as they grow and ripen. You can buy melon bags, but it's much cheaper to use old pantyhose, an old T-shirt, or any type of mesh netting to create a sling that you can attach to the trellis. Besides saving space, growing melons vertically with slings helps protect your melons from pests and fungal disease.

# Plant a garbage can irrigation system for your tomato garden.

Tomatoes are vigorous growers that need a lot of water to really thrive (about 2" a week). This ingenious hack creates a simple drip-irrigation system that will keep your tomatoes watered even in arid areas, using a regular garbage can and mesh wire to create a tomato cage.

## Materials:

- Power drill
- Standard 32-gallon plastic garbage can
- Compost
- Tomato plants
- Wire mesh (chicken wire will work) with posts for support

## Instructions:

1. Drill several holes in the bottom of the can, then another row of holes about 12" from the bottom of the can.

2. Bury the can up to the first row of holes and add a few inches of compost to the bottom of the can.

3. Plant your tomatoes next to the can, then build your tomato cage using the wire mesh so the tomatoes are enclosed. (This is not shown in the image.)

4. To water your tomatoes, add water to the garbage can without getting the tomato leaves wet. As the plants grow, they will draw moisture as needed from the can, which acts like a reservoir no matter how dry your conditions are.

# 183

## Create a wire-and-moss planter on top of old tree stumps or poles.

This is a great way to transform an old tree stump or large pole into a planter without any cutting involved—all you need is wire mesh, some screws or nails, and sphagnum moss. To create the planter, shape the wire to fit the top of your stump or pole, then fasten it in place with screws or nails. Soak the sphagnum moss and line the inside of the wire with a thick layer of wet moss. Fill the container with potting soil, and you're ready to plant. You can plant in the top of this container and in the sides, entirely obscuring the wire and moss container. Once planted, make sure you keep your container moist so the moss doesn't dry out.

# 184

## Maximize your potato crop with a potato tower made of chicken wire and stone.

Growing potatoes in buckets or bags is a great option for gardeners who want potatoes but have limited room. This idea represents the next level up: creating larger vertical potato planters from chicken wire, rebar, soil, and straw. This method allows you to grow larger amounts of potatoes. Better yet, harvest is a snap.

### Materials:

- Seed potatoes
- Chicken wire up to 4' wide and 5' long
- Zip ties
- Pliers and wire cutters
- 2 3½" pieces of rebar
- Straw (one or two bales)
- Potting soil

## Instructions:

1. Start your seed potatoes. For large seed potatoes, cut them into pieces, leaving at least one "eye" on each piece. Let them sit out for 24 hours on a paper towel to dry.

2. Form your potato towers by rolling your wire into a circle between 18" and 24" in diameter, cutting as needed to fit. Fasten the wire together with zip ties, or you can use pliers to twist the wire around itself.

3. Stand the wire cage upright in your growing space. Thread the rebar through the wire squares, then pound the rebar into the ground to secure the potato towers.

4. Line the inside of the tower with straw, leaving an opening in the middle. This first layer should be about 12" tall.

5. Add potting soil to the center.

6. Plant your first potatoes in the soil and cover with straw.

7. Repeat with layers of straw and soil until the tower is filled up.

8. Cap the tower with a thick layer of straw.

9. To maintain, give your tower lots of water. When you're ready to harvest, you can work your way down, harvesting a few potatoes at a time, or you can open the whole tower and harvest all the potatoes at the same time.

# 185

## Convert your old wine bottles into cool garden-bed edging.

To create a wine bottle edging, save up enough bottles to cover the space you need, then bury them upside down with only the bottom 6" or so of the bottle sticking up. Don't worry if it's not perfect—wine bottle edging is meant to be eclectic and funky (especially since you'll probably be using all different types of bottles, unless you really, really like one particular kind of wine!). If a bottle breaks or becomes cloudy, it's easy to replace a single bottle. And make sure to check your bottles in the spring, replacing any that might have broken over the winter.

# 186

## Make plant row markers with stones and paint.

This is a fun project you can do with your kids and a few tubes of regular acrylic paint. The idea is to create garden row markers you can use to help label your plants, but beyond that, there really aren't rules. Start by gathering some decorative stones with flat surfaces. If you can't find any, you can always buy river rocks from a local garden center. Set up a painting area and let everyone paint their stones, including the plant name and some bright and interesting accents and colors. The painted rocks should withstand at least one season in your garden...and then you can repaint them or create new ones!

# 187

## Build your own bird feeder.

Adding a few bird feeders to your garden can invite
all types of birds to enjoy your space. While you can,
of course, purchase really nice bird feeders,
you can also make your own with just a plastic
16- or 20-ounce bottle and a few wooden spoons or
dowels. Simply cut small holes in the bottle so you can
slide the dowels or spoons through the bottle, making sure to keep
them balanced. A spot of glue will hold the spoons in place. Then cut
a hole above the spoon or dowel just large enough for a few seeds to
trickle out. And that's it! Fill your impromptu bird feeder with seed
and hang it from a hook or branch with a sturdy length of string.

# 188

## Supplement your tomatoes with baking soda.

Gardeners have relied on baking soda for decades as a natural anti-
septic and antifungal agent, but when it comes to tomatoes, this inexpensive and widely available ingredient offers something else: better
taste. Baking soda is an alkaline substance, meaning it has a pH greater
than 7. When you supplement tomatoes with a mixture of 1 teaspoon
of baking soda and 1 gallon of water, and water as needed (depending
on the size of your plant), it helps concentrate the natural sugars in
the fruit. The end result is that your tomatoes are sweeter at harvest.
You can also use baking soda as a foliar spray, which will help prevent
or kill blights and mildews that attack tomato leaves.

## 189

# Create a simple fountain with a container, river rocks, and a pump.

This may be the simplest fountain possible: A simple copper pipe rises from a bed of river rocks, sending water splashing merrily back down into the container. To create this fountain, you'll need a container, a pump, a length of copper tube, and river rocks, plus a power drill and epoxy for assembly. Begin by drilling a hole in the side of the container for the pump's power supply (use a ceramic or glass drill bit if you're drilling through ceramic). Set the pump in the container and position the copper tube so it rests next to the pump, then thread the pump's plastic tubing up the copper. Now seal the power cord hole with epoxy. Carefully pile rocks in the container to hold the copper tube in place. Fill with water and turn on! If you want extra noise, bend the copper tube like a cane so the water spills out and splashes on the rocks below.

# 190

## Use cascading flowers to give your broken containers a second life.

Broken ceramic isn't useless ceramic! Instead of tossing your old ceramic, try recycling it into a beautiful display of overflowing flowers. All you have to do is lay the broken container sideways on the ground, with the open side facing up. Mound potting soil inside the container through the opening, then plant with your favorite cascading plants or flowers. To complete the effect, plant more of the same type of plant at the mouth of the container, so it looks like the plants are literally spilling from the mouth of your ceramic.

# 191

## Make a wind chime with old keys and silverware.

Have you got a "junk drawer" full of old keys you don't know what to do with? Or maybe some old silverware lurking in a cabinet somewhere? How about turning those old bits into a whimsical set of wind chimes? This DIY project couldn't be easier; you can easily complete it in an hour. Simply hang the old keys and silverware from a stick or piece of bamboo by decorative string or monofilament line. Try painting them first to add a splash of musical color. Hang your homemade wind chimes on your porch or in your garden and enjoy the sound of the breeze tinkling through the metal.

# 192

## Create a "bean fort" to grow beans and provide a play space.

This great hack combines two awesome things: a place to grow beans and a fort for kids to play in. Bean forts can be built from any type of wood, as long as it's strong enough to support growing beans. You can use trellis from your local big-box store, bamboo, or even branches you collect from your property. Assembling the fort requires only twine or strong string.

### Materials:

- Sections of wood trellis or long sticks
- String or twine
- Landscape fabric
- Bean plants

### Instructions:

1. Plan your fort shape based on your materials. You can make a simple, pointy, tent-style fort from straight sticks or poles, while trellis can be used to create a boxy fort.

2. Assemble the fort by sinking your wall material a few inches into the soil and tying pieces together. If you're using a trellis to create a boxy fort, enlist some help to lift the roof into place and use the string or twine to tie it to the walls.

3. Lay landscape fabric on the ground inside the fort.

**4.** Plant your beans along the outside walls.

**5.** Your fort will look barren at first, but the beans will quickly grow up the sides with proper watering and feeding. As they grow, tie the beans to the fort structure until you have a fully covered fort. At harvest time, you can easily pick hanging beans and enjoy!

# 193

## Put your old mirrors to work in the garden to add dimension and space.

Well-designed gardens are about more than plants. They include elements to add texture, dimension, elevation, and character. One easy way to catch your visitors' attention is with mirrors. Instead of throwing out that old mirror, try mounting it on a fence or tree, in a location where the mirror will reflect the best features of your garden. If you don't have any old mirrors, you can often find them at thrift stores. When visitors enter your garden, they'll do a double take at the double vision your mirror creates.

# 194

## Use stair risers to create a terraced garden.

Terraced gardens not only save space; they look cool too. If you don't want to go through the trouble of building a terraced garden, or you want something you can take down at the end of the season, this inventive terraced garden is a great choice. Created from regular stair risers and window boxes, it'll give you plenty of growing room, and it can be easily dissembled in the fall.

### Materials:

- 2 stair risers (you can purchase these precut from a lumberyard or big-box store)
- Circular saw or handsaw
- 2 2x4s + 2 pieces of 2x4 equal in length to the window boxes
- Long screws
- Window boxes (1 for each "step" you plan to create)
- Soil

### Instructions:

1. Determine how many window boxes you want to plant, then cut the stair risers to fit with a circular saw or handsaw.

2. Measure and cut the 2x4s so they are long enough to support the top of the stair risers and the boards are flush with the top of the risers.

3. Use two long screws per side to fasten the 2x4s to the risers.

4. Fasten the shorter boards across the top and bottom of the risers, thereby connecting the risers.

5. Carefully lift the terrace into place. It should be sturdy, with supports on the bottom and top.

6. Place the window boxes on each riser.

7. Fill window boxes with soil and plant.

8. At the end of the season, to disassemble your terraced garden, you can remove the screws holding the shorter boards in place, then stack the riser and support assembly in storage until the next growing season.

# 195

## Turn your tree stumps into flower containers.

Removing tree stumps is either very difficult or very expensive work. This hack transforms them into incredible planters. If you have a large stump in your yard or garden, use an ax or chainsaw (electric is fine) to hollow out a container in the top of the stump. The deeper and bigger the hole, the more soil and plants you can fit into the stump. When you're done, you can add container soil to the hole and plant in it. Be careful, however, when watering this type of container—your stump container will not drain quickly. If you live in an area with a lot of rain, consider drilling a hole from the inside of your stump container to the outside, so excess water can easily drain away.

# 196

## Use buttermilk paint to create mossy rocks.

Mossy rocks add a weathered, fantastical dimension to your garden. In some places, moss grows easily and naturally—but for most people, if you want that aged mossy look, you have to give the moss a little help. To create your own mossy rocks, mix up a batch of "moss paint" and coat rocks with it. Moss paint is a combination of one part buttermilk to one part moss (you can use any moss you find growing in your area). Put this combination into a blender and blend until it's smooth and paintable. Paint this mixture onto stones (in a shady place) and spritz with water for a few weeks to keep it moist and encourage the moss to grow. Once the moss has come in, occasionally mist it to keep it green and vibrant.

# 197

## Create instant path lighting with LED light strips.

Path lighting is more than pretty; it's also a safety feature that helps people navigate your garden at night. Professional path lighting can be expensive and may not be necessary to achieve a beautiful effect. Instead, you can invest in strip LED lighting and lay it along the path edge. In recent years, manufacturers have introduced weatherproof strip lights meant as holiday lights. Inexpensive compared to low-voltage landscaping lights, LED light strips are also simple to install. You just have to provide a weatherproof electrical source and lay or clip the lights in place. For extra convenience, add a timer to the outlet.

## 198

### Make a drip-irrigation hose with an old garden hose.

Drip irrigation is an excellent strategy to reduce your water consumption and provide moisture, especially for transplants of tender crops like lettuce. This smart hack converts an old garden hose into a drip-irrigation watering hose at a fraction of the cost of premade drip hoses. Simply take an old hose and, using either a drill with a very small bit or a sharp tack, puncture holes along the length of the hose—the more the better. Seal off one end of the hose with an inexpensive hose end cap. Hook it up to a water source and test your hose to see how much water pressure you need to make it function. When you've got enough holes and good flow, bury the hose near your plants.

# 199

## Build an instant garden bench from cinder block and fence posts.

This simple garden bench is the ultimate in cheap, durable, and fast seating. Made from fence posts and cinder blocks, you can get all the materials you need at a local big-box store and assemble the whole bench in an afternoon.

### Materials:

- 6 (4" x 4" x 8') pressure-treated fence posts
- 14 standard cinder blocks
- Masonry glue
- Epoxy sealer or paint for posts
- Cement primer and paint (optional)
- Pillows

### Instructions:

1. It's best to build this in place, so you're not moving cinder blocks when you're done. Prepare the site and measure the distance between the bench sides. If you're using 8' posts, measure your 8' bench, then mark 10" in on either side. This is where the outside edge of your blocks will be located.

**2.** Form the bench sides by stacking cinder blocks, with two side by side, three blocks tall, and using the masonry glue to fasten them together. You can situate the bottom two rows of blocks with the holes facing out, or with the holes facing vertically to create a solid face. The top row of blocks should be positioned on their sides, leaving the holes visible.

**3.** Position the two remaining blocks upright on the top layer (to form the anchors for the back of the bench) and glue in place.

**4.** If you're going to paint the blocks, now is the time.

**5.** Let the masonry glue set. While it's setting, use epoxy or paint to coat and protect the fence posts. Let this dry.

**6.** When the fence posts are dry, slide four of them through the holes in the blocks to create the bench seat. Slide the remaining two through the upright blocks to form the seat back.

**7.** Cover the posts with pillows for comfort, and you're done!

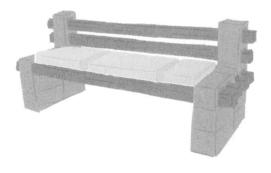

# 200

## Make a DIY compost bin from an old garbage can.

Rich, organic compost is black gold for gardeners. The basic concept of composting is simple: Mix different types of organic material, either in a pile or a large container, and let it decompose into a soil amendment. While you can buy composting systems that provide the compost bin, you can make your own compost bin at home for around $30, or the cost of a sturdy round garbage can.

### Materials:

- Power drill with ½" drill bit
- Large, round outdoor plastic garbage can with lid
- Bungee cord
- A few bricks or cinder blocks

### Instructions:

1. Drill about two dozen holes in the garbage can sides and bottom. These holes are essential for good ventilation.

2. Fill the can with a mix of green (e.g., clippings, leaves, kitchen scraps) and brown (e.g., shredded paper or cardboard, dried leaves) material. Only fill it about halfway full so the can isn't too heavy to manage.

3. Lightly moisten the mix. You want it to be wet but not soaking.

4. Cover the can and use the bungee cord to secure the lid in place.

5. Place the can on the bricks or cinder blocks to ensure good circulation on all sides.

6. Once a week, roll the can over a few times on the ground to mix the compost.

7. Check your compost after two weeks. Depending on where your can is located, the compost may be done in as little as two weeks. Finished compost is mostly broken down, with few recognizable ingredients left.

## 201

# Try square foot gardening to maximize your small space.

Popularized by retired engineer Mel Bartholomew, square foot gardening swept the gardening world when it was introduced. This method allows gardeners to intensively plant even very small spaces—usually 4' x 4'—and dramatically increase their yields. It starts with a raised garden bed filled with soil. To design your garden, lay out PVC pipe or rope in a grid on the dirt, creating squares of 1' on each side. In a 4' x 4' garden, you'll be able to measure sixteen squares. Next, plant each square with a different crop. You can get one tomato or pepper plant in each square, or plant your squares with lettuce, cabbage, or root vegetables. Once planted, care for your garden like any vegetable garden, harvesting your produce at the peak of ripeness.

# 202

## Convert your old teapots into a whimsical foundation.

This project converts an old teapot into a lively water feature for your garden. When it comes to the actual shape and character of the fountain, let your imagination run wild—you can use a bird bath, copper tray, old tub, or even another teapot for the bottom catch basin.

### Materials:

- Catch basin
- Drill with large metal bit
- Clear plastic tubing, long enough to run as a supply line from your catch basin up to the teapot
- Epoxy or waterproof caulk
- ½" copper tube for mounting the teapot
- Teapot (if you're using a metal teapot, you'll need a drill with a metal bit)
- Small water pump, like an aquarium pump

### Instructions:

1. Prepare the catch basin by drilling a hole in the bottom for the supply line, then feed the supply line through and seal the hole with waterproof caulk or epoxy. (If your catch basin is ceramic, plan to hide the water-supply line where it emerges from the basin.) Leave enough supply line in the catch basin to connect to the pump, and ensure the line outside of the basin is long enough to connect your basin to the teapot.

**2.** Prepare your copper support pipe by measuring how tall you want your fountain to be, then adding up to 2' in length so you can drive the pipe into the ground.

**3.** Measuring up from the bottom of the pipe, determine where the ground level will be, then drill a hole large enough for the plastic tube.

**4.** Fasten the teapot to the copper tube, either by drilling through the bottom of a metal teapot and using caulk or epoxy to attach it, or you can use silicone glue to attach the copper tube to the teapot.

**5.** Assemble the fountain by carefully driving the copper tube into the ground, making sure you don't knock the teapot off. If the ground is hard, dig a hole, then place the pipe and backfill with dirt.

**6.** Position the catch basin below the pot, then thread the supply line up the copper pipe and into the teapot.

**7.** Fill the basin with water and plug in the pump to activate it.

# 203

## Create underground drip irrigators with 2-liter bottles.

Plants that are watered directly at the root zone tend to grow faster and better, since they put less effort into growing an extensive root system. This ingenious hack transforms a regular 2-liter bottle into an underground drip-irrigation reservoir that will supply water directly to your plant's root zone. To create your own, simply poke a dozen or two small holes in a 2-liter bottle (make sure you still have the cap). Next, bury the 2-liter bottle right alongside the root zone of a plant, leaving the spout exposed, then fill it with water and secure it firmly with the cap. Water will seep from the container into the soil, meaning you won't have to worry about watering again until the bottle is empty. To refill, just unscrew the cap and fill it with fresh water.

# Chapter 4

# INDOOR GARDENING

# 204

## Display plants in groups to create a healthy microclimate.

The most popular houseplants are often from the tropics or subtropics, where they naturally thrive in high humidity, warmth, and steady rain. These conditions can be hard to create in most residential homes—but this simple hack is a step in the right direction. Just like people, plants also "breathe," and through a process called "transpiration," they give off water through pores in their leaves. When you're displaying plants, group them in clusters of three or more to create a microclimate among the plants themselves, with higher humidity and shelter from drafts. Better yet, grouped plants look lusher and fuller, so this is really a win-win for you and your plants.

# 205

## Use mayonnaise as a plant polish.

This is a trick interiorscapers use to make their houseplants and interior plants literally shine, without spending a lot of money on expensive leaf-shine sprays. Simply put a little mayonnaise on a damp cloth and rub it into your plant's leaves. The cloth will remove dust, and the oil in the mayonnaise will polish up those leaves into a glossy shine. This is especially effective on big-leaved, striking plants.

## 206

### Create a windowsill herb garden with Mason jars.

If you have a few old Mason or Ball jars around, plus some seed packets for herbs, you're already more than halfway to creating a farmhouse-style windowsill herb garden. Just add container soil to the jars, plant the seeds, and line up the jars on a sunny windowsill. The kitchen is a great location, because it's usually warmer and more humid. Use decorative labels on your jars for a nice display. You'll need to be very careful watering, because there is no drainage in the jars, but since you're growing in clear glass, you'll be able to easily see how wet the soil is. Only water sparingly, and never let water collect in the bottom of the jar to create mud.

## 207

### Take compass direction into account when placing plants.

This free hack can make all the difference between a healthy plant and one that's struggling. Unlike outside plants, your indoor plants only get as much light as your windows allow. And not all windows are equal. East-facing windows get gentle morning sun until about midday, making them perfect for plants that like dappled shade or mid-range light. West-facing windows offer stronger late-afternoon sun, so are appropriate for plants that can handle more heat. North-facing windows will never receive direct sunlight, so are good for shade-loving plants. And finally, south-facing windows get a full dose of afternoon sun and are best for full-sunlight plants.

## 208

### Plant ginger for a beautiful houseplant.

Ginger grows as an underground rhizome; the part we eat is actually the root of the plant. If you have ginger left over, place it in water or a plastic bag with a damp paper towel (leave the bag slightly open for air circulation) at room temperature. In several weeks, you'll see white roots emerge, along with a green sprout. At this point, you can transplant your ginger to a container, making sure to keep the sprout pointing up. Bury the whole rhizome and water the ginger gently. Ginger likes to grow in a bright, warm, and humid spot. You can harvest your ginger in about ten months.

# 209

## Plant your romaine lettuce stems for new lettuce plants.

It is surprisingly easy to sprout romaine stems at home. To grow your own romaine in water, save the stem end of the lettuce after you've used it. (This tip works best if you leave about 2" of leaves on the stem.) Place the lettuce stem-side down in a dish of clean water. Put it on a bright but not sunny windowsill and refresh the water periodically. You'll soon see new lettuce emerge from the top of the stem. You can harvest these leaves directly as they emerge and are still small, or you can transplant the lettuce into a container with well-drained potting soil and grow larger heads of romaine.

# 210

## Use pebble trays to increase humidity.

Indoor gardeners are often looking for ways to increase humidity around their plants, whether it's spritzing them frequently, grouping them together, or using this old trick. A pebble tray is exactly what it sounds like: a small tray of pebbles or decorative rocks filled with water. The evaporation from the pebble tray placed near your plants will add some moisture to your growing zone and make your plants happy. If you want to make the tray decorative, treat it like a miniature Japanese garden and display ceramics or mini statues.

# 211

## Sprout old carrot tops in water to start a carrot garden.

Carrots are just one of the many grocery store vegetables you can easily sprout at home. Better yet, you can sprout carrots and still use the carrot in the kitchen. To spout a carrot, save the top and place it in a shallow dish of clean water so the water only just barely covers the bottom of the cut piece. Leave the dish in a bright but not directly sunny place, and refresh the water periodically. Soon, feathery foliage will sprout from the carrot top. When the foliage is a few inches tall, you can transplant the carrot into a container. Make sure to choose a deep container with enough room for the carrot to develop under the soil level.

## 212

### Glue air plants to a corkboard to make a living wall hanging.

Air plants are a fantastic group of plants that have evolved to grow clinging to trees up in the air. The vast majority of these plants are in the *Tillandsia* genus, and they come in all kinds of shapes. Some look like spiky hair, some like coral, and still others like curling green squid. Growing air plants inside is as simple as spraying them with water every so often, as they don't need dirt or containers. When it comes to displaying air plants, this cool corkboard hack makes the most of their airborne nature and displays them how they look best—in groups. All you need is a corkboard and a selection of air plants, plus some glue. Just glue the stem end of the plants to the corkboard and hang it up. Be sure to pick waterproof glue and don't get any on the leaves.

## 213

### Add food coloring to water to transform white cut flowers.

This neat trick is sometimes used to demonstrate to students how plants take up water through their stems. Put a bouquet of light-colored cut flowers in a vase of water that has been treated with food coloring. Over time, the flowers will absorb the coloring, and their petals will transform into different hues of the rainbow. This works particularly well with geraniums, but you can use any light-colored flower. Flowers with dark petals are typically too pigmented already for you to notice the difference.

# 214

## Construct a hanging air plant garden to avoid messy watering.

Growing hanging plants indoors can be tricky—you either have to move them to the sink when watering to protect your floors against runoff, or you have to use containers with no drainage holes and risk an overwatering disaster. And, if you have a lot of plants, it can get expensive to build up your collection of hanging pots. Skip the mess (and the price tag!) by using old Mason jars (or other decorative tins) to create a hanging garden of bromeliads and air plants (*Tillandsia*).

### Materials:

- 3 or 4 small Mason jars (or other decorative tins)
- Hanging wire with a loop
- Sphagnum moss
- Bromeliads or air plants, one for each container

### Instructions:

1. Safely secure the containers to your hanging wire. For glass containers like Mason jars, you can secure them in macramé nets or tie the wire onto the rim of the glass. A dab of epoxy where the metal meets the glass can help ensure a safe connection. For metal tins or other containers, puncture a hole in the rim and loop the wire through it. Make sure to use the full length of the wire so it hangs correctly.

2. Fill the containers with sphagnum moss.

3. Secure the plants in the moss.

4. When you're done planting, hang your new vertical air garden from a ceiling hook in a bright place.

5. Care for your plants as necessary. For example, misting should be enough for the *Tillandsia* air plants, but make sure to keep a bit of water in the "cup" of your bromeliad. You won't need to fill the containers with water, though—these plants are designed to thrive hanging in the air and don't take up much water, if any, through their roots.

## 215

### Get a second use from your cooking water!

If you like to cook, here's a neat trick to get the most from your healthy veggies, eggs, and even pasta: Reuse your cooking water to water your houseplants. When you boil vegetables, eggs, and pasta, some of the nutrients from the food leach into the water during cooking. Normally, you'd pour that down the sink without a second thought. Instead, set aside the cooking container, let the water cool to room temperature, and use it to water your indoor plants. Research has shown that valuable minerals like potassium, calcium, and magnesium readily leach into cooking water, along with an array of vitamins including vitamin B. Your plants will appreciate these added nutrients just as much as you will.

# 216

## Create a moss pole for your vines.

Some popular houseplants are naturally climbers, including certain philodendron, monstera, and pothos vines. If you want them to achieve their maximum potential, give them something to climb, like a moss pole.

### Materials:

- Sphagnum moss
- PVC-coated mesh
- Wire ties or some other sturdy wire

### Instructions:

1. Begin by soaking the sphagnum moss in water for at least 15 minutes. While it's soaking, cut off a piece of mesh large enough to roll into a 5" cylinder. Lay the mesh flat and fill it tightly with moss.

2. When you have plenty of moss, pull the edges of the mesh together to remake the cylinder and use the wire to stitch it closed.

3. To plant, bury the moss poll in a container and train your vine to attach to the pole with plant ties. If you're growing something heavy, add rocks to the bottom of the pot so the pole won't get top-heavy.

# 217

## Use grow bulbs in dim corners to provide more light.

Indoor gardeners are often in a constant battle for light. Even moving a plant a few feet away from a window can result in a dramatic drop in light intensity, which can be challenging for all but the most shade-tolerant plants. This simple hack is possible thanks to recent improvements in the technology of grow bulbs. To help your indoor plants thrive, consider adding some grow lights to the growing area. You can buy LED grow lights relatively inexpensively, including bulbs that clamp to desks or shelves. Alternatively, even adding a regular fluorescent bulb can help—just position it close enough to the plants to bathe them in light.

# 218

## Mulch your indoor containers too!

Mulch is brown gold for outside gardeners, but few people think of mulch for indoor containers. But why not? Your indoor plants will enjoy all the same benefits mulch offers to your outside garden, including better water retention in the soil and the slow decay of the organic matter boosting your soil. Even better, you won't need much mulch for containers. If you want to give this a try, add a layer about 2" thick to your large containers, and a thinner layer to your smaller containers. Once you've added the mulch, you can take care of your plants just like normal, although you may not need to water as much.

# 219

## Grow your tropical plants in the bathroom.

If your houseplants had to pick a favorite room in the house, most of them would immediately pick the bathroom. Bathrooms tend to be warmer, with higher humidity and less draft than any other room in the house. If you have a window in the bathroom, even better—a bright, warm bathroom is tropical plant heaven. So if you're having trouble keeping plants alive in your main living areas, why not move a few containers into the bathroom? This one simple move might be the difference between pots with brown and dying plants and vibrant greenery—and your bathroom will look great too.

# 220

## Quarantine new plants to protect your collection.

The trip from seed to the local garden center's display can be a long one for most plants, involving greenhouses, vehicles, warehouses, and finally the garden center itself. Along the way, there are plenty of opportunities for plants to pick up nasty pests and all sorts of diseases you don't want to bring into your collection. To prevent contamination, when you're buying new plants, it's always a good idea to quarantine them for two weeks or so before bringing them into close contact with your healthy plants. During quarantine, inspect them regularly for signs of infestation, and treat any problems accordingly.

# 221

## Sprout your avocado pits with toothpicks and a glass of water.

If you've ever cut an avocado open, you're familiar with the large pit encased in the green fruit prized for guacamole and on toast. This pit, which is really a giant seed, can be sprouted with a few simple supplies you likely have in your kitchen cupboard. According to the California Avocado Commission, here's the best way to do it:

- Wash the pit well.

- Insert three toothpicks into the pit and suspend it over a glass of water, with the broad end down and submerged about an inch.

- Keep it in a warm, bright place but not in direct sunlight.

- Refresh and refill the water as needed.

- Wait 2–6 weeks for your new avocado plant to sprout!

## 222

### Create a vertical hanging herb garden with a shoe organizer.

Short on space but still want to grow fresh herbs? This simple DIY herb garden transforms a regular canvas shoe organizer into a hanging herb garden. Once completed, you can hang it near any window or on your balcony. If you're making a version

to go outside, just add potting soil to the canvas pouches, then plant with herbs. For an inside version, line the pouches with plastic bags before adding soil. But be careful! If you do this, the pouches won't drain, so be cautious when watering so you don't drown the herbs.

# 223

## Plant your scallion bases after trimming.

Despite what you may have heard, a scallion and a spring onion are not the same thing. Spring onions are immature bulb onions that, if left to grow long enough, will form a small, tender bulb. Scallions—sometimes called green onions—grow with a straight stem all the way down to the roots. Scallions are common in many types of cuisine and often sold in bunches in the supermarket. Similar to almost any veggie that is sold with roots attached, you can easily sprout and grow scallions yourself. All you need to do is submerge the bottom inch of a scallion in clean water, then change the water every few days. Keep the jar in a bright place, and snip the green scallion tops as they emerge.

# 224

## Vacuum up pests from your plants.

One of the easiest pest control approaches has nothing to do with toxic sprays or chemicals. The next time you're vacuuming, especially with a handheld model, check out your plants as well. If you see pests like spiders or mealybugs, vacuum the little monsters away. It's true you won't get all of them, but if you get into the habit of checking every time you vacuum, you'll be able to keep the population in control and delay the transition to more serious pest control measures.

# 225

## Split up supermarket herb plants to double their output.

In recent years, more and more supermarkets have started selling potted herbs. It's common now to find potted basil, oregano, chives, and thyme in the produce section. The advantage to buying potted herbs is that you get fresh herbs for much longer than if you just buy the harvested leaves—you can snip basil off a plant for weeks. The issue, however, is that you'll inevitably end up cutting off so many leaves that the plant dies. If you want to double how long your potted herbs last, consider dividing the herbs right when you get home. (Your herbs will likely have more than one main stem, so they can be easily divided.) Water both pots and choose one to snip while the other grows and recovers, waiting for its turn to enhance your salads and dishes with the bright taste of fresh herbs.

# 226
## Invest in a light meter
## (and learn how much light your plants need).

Many plants with high light requirements suffer inside, while even "shade-loving" plants may stretch if they don't get access to decent light. Light intensity is typically measured in lux; 320–500 lux is office lighting, while direct sunlight can measure in at a whopping 100,000 lux. For plants, the following lux levels match up with common light requirements:

- **Low light** = up to 2,500 lux
- **Medium light** = 2,500–10,000 lux
- **Bright** = 10,000–20,000 lux
- **Full sun** = 20,000+ lux

The best way to know your light levels is to invest in a lux meter, which you can find at your local garden center or online. You might be surprised with your readings at first, but the information will allow you to make better choices about where to put certain plants.

# 227

## Keep a mister around to boost humidity.

Indoor air is notoriously dry, especially for the tropical plants many people love to grow. In fact, in the tropics, it's not uncommon for plants to experience 60 percent or more humidity on steamy-hot days. By contrast, humidity inside your home can be as low as 30 percent. This hack helps you provide plenty of humidity with almost no effort. All you need to do is keep a mister bottle filled with water in your growing area and get in the habit of misting your plants every few days. This will also keep their leaves clean and dust-free. If remembering to mist is difficult, keep your mister next to your watering can and give plants a spritz with every watering.

# 228

## Plant your pineapple tops.

The pineapple is the only edible bromeliad, so every time you buy a pineapple with its spiky leaves, you're also buying a ready-to-plant bromeliad. Next time you get a pineapple, instead of throwing away the top with the leaves attached, try planting the top instead. You can put it in water, but there's really no reason. As a bromeliad, pineapples are watered from the top and collect water in the cups of their leaves. So plant it in dirt, burying the top to the point where the leaves begin, then fill the central cup in the middle of the plant with water and put it in a bright spot.

## 229

### Add LED lights to containers to create simple indoor fairy gardens.

Fairy gardens are all about light and whimsy. If you want to create an indoor fairy garden, pick up some inexpensive strings of miniature LED lights and wrap them around or string them through your indoor houseplants. The wires are so small as to be almost invisible—until night comes and they illuminate your plants with mysterious points of light. Just one note of caution: Make sure you can store the LED battery pack outside the container, so it doesn't get wet when you're watering.

## 230

### Let your plants help purify your indoor air.

Thanks to research conducted at NASA, we know that indoor plants act like living filters that can clean polluted indoor air by trapping volatile organic compounds in their tissues. The catch? You need a *lot* of plants per square foot to achieve the same results the NASA scientists discovered. Still, even if you can't stuff your living space with plants, adding even a few plants will help. The plants that have been shown to best clean indoor air include popular favorites like mother-in-law's tongue, elephant's ear, peace lilies, spider plants, and indoor palm trees.

# 231

## Train your pothos vine to climb around your walls.

In nature, pothos vines hardly resemble the cute and hardy little vines tumbling out of your indoor container. In their natural habitat, pothos are aggressive climbers that can easily scramble up huge palms and hardwoods, draping them with foot-long variegated leaves. You can bring this same jungle vibe into your home by training your pothos to grow up walls and even along ceilings. The vines are lightweight and can be hung from small hooks as they grow; their roots won't damage your walls. In a bright room with good light, plus steady water and fertilizer for the main plant, you can train a single vine to create a "pothos wall" or a living crown molding.

## 232

### Disguise those ugly views with tall indoor plants.

Unfortunately, not every window looks out onto an idyllic glade or sparkling lake—sometimes you're just staring at your neighbor's wall or right into their windows. Instead of hiding these windows behind blinds you keep closed, how about putting that light to work and moving a row of palms, bamboo, or even ficus in front of the window to create a beautiful, living barrier? This works best if you use just one type of plant all in matching containers, so you're not accidentally bringing attention to the window, but instead are creating a simple and attractive display that will brighten your room and hide that ugly view.

## 233

### Place herbs in containers with tall plants.

Gardeners who cook will love this creative approach to tucking some herbs into their existing indoor plant spaces. If you have tall plants, like a ficus tree, trim away the bottom leaves and branches to expose the main trunk, then plant a bed of herbs around the base of the plant. If you don't want to dig into the container soil, you can also just set potted herbs on the soil, rotating them as you use the herbs. And don't worry about hurting your taller plant— you may even be helping it as you remove leaves that were starved for light and allow the plant to concentrate on its new growth.

## 234

### Revive indoor plants by giving them an outdoor vacation.

Life can be hard for indoor plants—too dry, too cold, not enough light, and stuck in a container it can't escape if your watering is uneven. If you have trouble keeping your houseplants thriving from season to season, take advantage of the natural benefit that rolls around every year: summer. If you time it right, you can move your indoor plants outside during the spring repotting season. The combination of a fresh container and summer sun is usually enough to stimulate fresh growth and prepare your plant for another winter indoors. Be careful, however, not to move your plant into direct sunlight too fast—most leafy plants will scorch if they transition too quickly. Instead, look for shady overhangs. At the end of the summer, check carefully for pests and treat the affected plants before bringing them in.

## 235

### Turn your old aquarium into a water garden.

Aquascaping is the practice of using an aquarium to plant a freshwater garden, usually without fish. The resulting tanks are vibrant with greenery and require less maintenance and effort than taking care of fish. An easy way to get started is to focus on epiphytes, or plants that don't need to be planted in the aquarium substrate (e.g., gravel) itself. Instead, these plants can be attached to features like rocks or wood with glue or thread. Once established, they'll spread through the aquarium. Good candidates include aquatic mosses, such as Java moss, and epiphytic aquatic ferns. Always use fresh, non-chlorinated water to plant your aquascape—these are aquatic plants and may be sensitive to chlorine. Also, feed your plants with a weak liquid fertilizer according to their labels.

## 236
### Create a sophisticated succulent dish with containers and moss.

Succulent dishes are a natural starting point for many indoor gardeners, thanks to being both easy to care for and beautiful. Unfortunately, it can also be expensive to buy premade dishes. However, with a few very basic supplies, you can create an "instant dish" on your own. All you need is a shallow dish and a selection of succulents in 2" containers (these are commonly sold in big-box retailers and garden centers), plus some sphagnum moss and pebbles. Line the bottom of the dish with pebbles, then artfully arrange the succulents on the pebble bed. Finally, pack the open spaces around the containers with the moss, hiding the unsightly containers. Water your succulents weekly, letting them dry between waterings. If one dies, just pop out that container and replace it.

## 237
### Let "understory" plants spruce up your shady rooms.

In a tropical ecosystem—where many of our favorite houseplants naturally come from—the "understory" is the part of the forest beneath the tree canopy. The understory has less light and more humidity and warmth than the forest canopy above, so the plants there have often developed huge leaves to soak up every available ray of sun. If you have a shady room, try growing understory plants that are naturally adapted to less light. These include monstera, philodendron, elephant's ears, and aroids.

## 238

### Welcome visitors to your home using feng shui and plants.

The Chinese concept of feng shui literally translates into "wind-water" and is all about achieving balance and directing positive energy in living spaces. In this school of thought, one of the most important areas of your home is your entrance. This is where people are welcomed in and where they first experience the energy of your home. While there are many elements to consider at your entrance, plants introduce the feng shui element of wood into your home and create a positive mood. Grouping plants at your front door is good feng shui, but make sure not to include dying or sick plants, or plants with spines or thorns that might be unwelcoming.

## 239

### Transform your unused fireplace into a plant showcase.

Tired of looking at your empty fireplace? Why not convert your fireplace into a showcase for plants? With their closed construction and durable materials like brick and stone, fireplaces are actually great for certain plants. You don't have to worry so much about water damage to the floor, and your plants will enjoy the protection and increased humidity from the small space. There are no real rules for planting in your fireplace, but if you wanted to really kick things up a notch, you could even run an extension cord into your fireplace and mount a halo-style LED light over your plants to provide plenty of light and create a stunning display.

## 240
# Mix your mother-in-law's tongue plant types to design interesting pots.

Sansevieria, sometimes called "mother-in-law's tongue" or "snake plants," make some of the best houseplants. They are easy to care for, with minimal water requirements, and are tolerant of a huge range of conditions, including dry air and drafts. These dramatic plants feature stiff, upright leaves and come in a variety of leaf patterns and colors. To level up your sansevieria game, group three or more variations of sansevieria together in containers, letting the contrast of their leaves and containers play off one another.

## 241
# Suspend containers from your walls with crochet slings.

Here's another cool way to use open wall space: Suspend containers from crochet slings resting against the wall or hanging from a simple coatrack. This works best if you use round, clear glass containers and grow epiphytes like bromeliads or air plants. These types of plants are low-maintenance and don't need extensive drainage or potting media, so you don't have to worry about damaging your wall with messy drainage. A simple spray bottle is all you'll need to take care of your living wall garden.

# 242

## Create a "living wall" indoors.

A "living wall" is a wall in your home that is draped with plants—often ferns or other tropical options, although you can use almost anything in a living wall. You can buy living wall systems, but these can be pricey—and the resulting walls can be beautiful but also require a lot of maintenance. This living wall, on the other hand, is much easier to build and maintain at a fraction of the cost of store-bought systems.

### Materials:

- Wire shelf or rack, flat and square
- Sturdy wall mounts and studs for the wire rack
- Plant container clips
- Containers (with no drainage holes, or you can seal the drainage holes with epoxy or caulk)
- Potting soil
- Plants

### Instructions:

1. Measure your wall and determine where you want your living wall located. The ideal location is near a window so your plants can enjoy bright, filtered light.

2. Mount the rack on the wall using four wall mounts connected to wall studs.

3. Fasten your plant clips to the containers.

4. Hang the containers from the wall. How far you place them from one another depends on what you're growing and how big your living wall is. Ideally, keep your containers close enough together that the plants will mostly obscure the containers.

5. Once you've planned where the containers will go, fill your containers with soil and your chosen plants.

6. Hang them up!

7. To maintain, regularly mist your living wall and water the plants as needed. Remember that these containers don't have drainage, so you'll need to be extra careful not to over-water your plants.

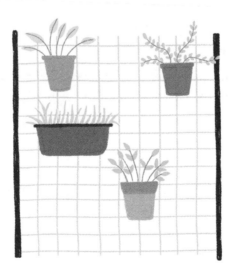

# 243

## Install a sturdy curtain rod to make a hanging garden.

Hanging gardens add elevation and a lush, living element to any room—and this hack makes it easy to hang multiple plants in the same location to create a canopy. You can try one of these two methods depending on your space:

- If you're dealing with a window that already has curtains, install a double curtain rod and use the outer rod for your plants and the inner rod for curtains.

- For windows with no existing rod, you can mount a rod just for plants. Look for rods that extend out from the wall a few inches, so you have more room for hanging plants.

  A few points to consider...

- Plants are much heavier than curtains! Make sure you're getting a rod that is rated to handle the weight of plant containers.

- Look for containers without drainage, so you can protect your floors.

- Consider hanging glass globes with air plants, which are easy to maintain with simple misting, are very lightweight, and still allow a view through the window.

- Frame your window by including trailing plants on the ends of the rod and smaller foliage plants between, making green "curtains."

# 244

## Turn your moss tower into a light display with a string of lights.

Moss towers are the best way to display larger climbing plants like monstera, some philodendron, and more mature pothos vines. This decorative hack takes your moss pole up a level, so it's just as attractive at night as it is during the day. Using a strand of holiday lights, gently wrap the moss pole from the bottom up. You can use colored lights for added effect, and if you're concerned about heat burying your plants, look for LED. Put the lights on a timer if you want them to turn on at the same time every night.

# 245

## Propagate pothos vines without cutting or trimming.

This method of propagating pothos vines—already one of the easiest houseplants to propagate—has one huge advantage over other techniques: You end up with a fully potted plant with no need for transplanting. This method uses two pots, including the container the original "mother" pothos lives in and a fresh pot filled with new container soil. For this to work, the mother plant should have vines long enough to reach into the second pot. Select one of these longer vines and strip off a few leaves at a node near the end, but don't damage the growing end. Bury the stripped part of the vine in the second container, leaving the growing tip with leaves exposed. Water as normal. New roots will emerge from the buried section, and in a few weeks, you'll be able to cut the umbilical vine.

# 246

## Make a decorative bottle garden.

Bottle gardens are basically terrariums in smaller and more inter-esting packages. They make really cool desktop accessories because they're small and don't leak water, and you're only limited by your imagination (and access to bottles) when it comes to the size and shape of your bottle garden.

### Materials:

- Pea gravel or decorative gravel
- Clean bottle with a cap; clear bottles work best to allow in lots of light
- Activated charcoal (you can find this in a garden center or online)
- Potting soil
- Chopsticks or long-handled and narrow tongs that can fit through the bottle opening (if your bottle has a wide mouth, you might be able to just reach inside with your hands)
- Plants

### Instructions:

1. Put a layer of pea gravel in the bottom of the bottle.

2. Next, add a thin layer of activated charcoal (this will help control odors).

3. Add the potting soil next, making this layer as deep as your bot-tle can accommodate while still leaving room for plants to grow.

4. Using the chopsticks, carefully place plants in the soil, starting with the smallest plants first.

5. Water gently, but don't allow water to swamp the gravel and charcoal.

6. Leave the bottle in a bright spot, with no cover, for two weeks. During this time, check the watering carefully until you've reached a balance, providing just enough water for the plants to thrive but not to soak the soil.

7. Cover the bottle and enjoy!

## 247

# Try a grow tent for serious indoor veggie farming.

There are various reasons people get serious about growing veggies indoors, including lack of land outside, inhospitable climate, and even avoiding foraging pests like deer. If you want to try your hand at growing amazing vegetables inside, invest in a grow tent. You can buy complete tents as kits, featuring everything from included grow lights to ventilation and instructions for how to get your tent set up and operating in a few hours. Smaller tents are available at 2' x 2', big enough for a single tomato plant. Once you have your tent set up, you can grow vegetables all year round.

## 248

### Glow up your interiorscape with LED containers.

Glowing containers are all the rage lately, and if you want the brightest and coolest ones, LED is the way to go. LED is much stronger than glow-in-the-dark paint, and when used in a plastic container, the lights will infuse the entire pot and cast a warm, colorful light. If you want to make one yourself, use the pot-within-a-pot approach: Get a large plastic container and a string of LED lights, then fasten the lights inside the container in a spiral pattern. Set another slightly smaller container with a plant in it inside the larger one (you might need to prop up this second container so it's level with the top of the outside container).

## 249

### Try bonsai for your narrow sills and small spaces.

Bonsai is the ancient Japanese art of growing miniaturized trees and plants in shallow trays and trimming them into traditional shapes. Creating your own bonsai is an artistic endeavor that requires careful training and patience. The good news is that you can buy bonsai in many garden centers today, and these miniature trees make perfect displays for narrow windowsills. Caring for your bonsai means watering it weekly and following the care instructions for that type of tree. And who knows? You might end up enjoying this mindful form of gardening and training your own miniature forest.

# 250

## Make your cuttings pretty: Hang them in decorative flasks while they sprout.

Taking cuttings is one of the easiest and best ways to get free plants—and many plants like pothos, philodendron, and umbrella plants root easily in plain water. If you're interested in taking cuttings with style, here's a clever idea: Root your cuttings in decorative glass flasks that you display instead of hiding away in some back room. A few hanging flasks with cuttings creates an unusual display of greenery, and when the cuttings are rooted, it's easy enough to transplant them into soil. Just be careful when you're hanging flasks to make sure the glass is well secured, and remember to change the water every few days to help the cuttings along.

# 251

## Try your hand with inexpensive mini orchids for jewel gardens.

Orchid growing can sound intimidating at first, with talk of special growing mixes, unique containers, and detailed instructions on how to care for the plants. In reality, growing great orchids is like anything else—it takes patience and learning. A good place to start is with the increasingly popular mini orchids. These jewel-like flowers are usually either phalaenopsis or dendrobium orchids and, thanks to their size, are easier to manage inside than their full-sized cousins. You can keep a mini orchid on a windowsill or desk, watering it thoroughly every week and then letting it dry. Once you've got the hang of the mini orchids, you can confidently start to buy the more expensive and bigger varieties.

## 252

### Use magnets to secure your mini pots to the refrigerator.

Why not grow some herbs right where you'll use them—in your kitchen? With some glue, magnets, and small containers, you can create a ready-to-eat herb garden on your refrigerator door in a few minutes. Just glue the magnets onto the containers with a strong epoxy, then fill the containers with dirt, and plant. Use small containers and young transplants to keep them from falling off. If you can't find smaller transplants, you can also grow directly from seed. These containers won't have drainage holes, so be careful while watering not to drown your plants.

## 253

### Create DIY night-lights with glow-in-the-dark paint and plants.

Here's a really cool project for a child's bedroom: Make glow-in-the-dark planters that also double as night-lights. To create your container, you can use any high-quality glow-in-the-dark paint, including spray paint. Coat your favorite container with several coats of paint—at least five might be necessary, maybe more. Let the paint dry thoroughly before you plant the container. To activate the glow-in-the-dark paint, leave the container in a very bright place through-out the day so it can soak up lots of light. When the sun goes down later, your paint should emit a nice glow. If you find that it's not glow-ing enough, considering adding some LED lights (see the hack "Glow up your interiorscape with LED containers" in this chapter).

# 254

## Place wheeled trays under big containers to make them easier to move.

Tired of dragging around huge containers or, worse, damaging your floors with trays? Put your plants on wheeled trays. You can find plastic wheeled trays at most garden centers or big-box stores, but you can use any decorative tray with wheels. When you're shopping, look for trays with higher-quality wheels—some of the cheaper trays will warp, or their wheels will freeze up in a matter of months, rendering the tray useless.

# 255

## Use humidifiers to create a moist environment for plants.

While dry indoor air is probably good for your computer and TV, not a lot of plants outside of cacti and succulents enjoy that air in the 30 percent humidity range. If you start finding brown tips on your leaves, or the edges of your leaves are turning brown and crispy, try adding a humidifier to the growing room. This little bit of extra humidity can make the difference between crispy and lush houseplants—and your skin will enjoy time spent around your plants as well.

## 256
## Always use spring water for your lucky bamboo!

Lucky bamboo—which is not really bamboo at all but a type of dracaena—is often marketed as the easiest houseplant to grow. There's a lot of truth to this, because after all, this is a plant that can survive wild swings in temperature and grows in plain water without any soil or drainage to worry about. There is one important caveat, however, to growing lucky bamboo well: They are sensitive to the type of water you use because they don't like chlorine. If you want your lucky bamboo to really thrive, always use spring water to water it to be sure it's chlorine-free.

## 257
## Don't repot those tropical plants too soon!

The bookshelves are thick with gardening books advising you to repot your houseplants every year. In some cases, this is great advice and your plants will thank you. But it's not always true, and knowing when you can (and should) skip a year or two can save you money and effort. The truth is that many tropical plants—including philodendron, monstera, aroids, and others—like to be a little pot-bound and will grow more quickly and vigorously if they are allowed to fill up their pot some. One easy way to tell if your plant can skip the yearly repotting is the presence of aerial roots. If you see roots emerging from the stem at one point, odds are this plant is accustomed to climbing trees and may not need to repotted right away.

# 258

## Improve your sleep with scented lavender in your bedroom.

Believe it or not, your sense of smell and your sleep patterns are more connected than you might think. According to the National Sleep Foundation, certain smells can help you relax faster and get to sleep more quickly. Lavender has long been known for its delicate aroma, and there is scientific evidence that it helps relax the nervous system and can improve sleep. If you'd like to see if it works for you, try moving a pot of lavender into your bedroom. At night before you go to sleep, brush the leaves gently to release the odor. Keep in mind, though, that your bedroom may be too dark to keep lavender thriving, so you will likely have to rotate the plant out or replace it after a few weeks.

# 259

## Repurpose old toys and ceramics in terrariums and funky displays.

Indoor gardeners don't have to give up on whimsy and fun—from fairy gardens to other themed gardens, you can create anything you can imagine in your interior growing space. The main difference is scale: Interior hardscaping is miniature compared to outdoor garden design. So next time you're cleaning out old toy or china cabinets, or even perusing a flea market or thrift shop, keep an eye out for props you can use in your own interiorscapes. Old toy trains and cars can be repurposed in terrariums; figurines and ceramics, combined with some LED lights, can transform a simple container into an enchanted forest. Best of all, you won't have to break the bank to add character to your plants.

# 260

## Mix some fake plants with your indoor plants for easy abundance.

Fake plants have come a long way, but they're still no substitute for the real thing. That said, they can be a great supplement. If you want to cut down on the time, hassle, and expense of caring for lots of real plants, consider buying some fake background plants and mixing them into your plant groupings. You might be surprised how few people actually notice that some of your plants aren't real when all they see is a lush green display. This trick gives you the best of both worlds—the benefits of living plants, and the reduced maintenance of fake ones.

## 261

### Turn your windowsill into a baby spinach farm.

Known for its nutritional punch, spinach is a perfect crop to grow indoors. Although you can grow it in individual containers, to get adequate spinach, it's better to use a foil or loaf pan. To create your spinach garden, fill the container with soil, then sow spinach seeds into the soil, spacing them 3" apart. Keep it gently watered; your spinach will sprout in about five days. While it's growing, keep it in a bright area, but don't expose it to direct sunlight. Spinach likes slightly cooler temperatures, so if your growing area gets above 80°F, you should relocate the tray. You can begin harvesting leaves as soon they are big enough to eat.

## 262

### Repurpose your old sponges as plant polishers.

After enough time inside, it's inevitable your plants will get dusty—there's no rain to wash away dirt. This dust won't harm your plants, but it does make them look dull and unhealthy instead of vibrant. Instead of buying dedicated plant wash, set aside an old sponge with your watering can and give the leaves a quick swipe when you water. If you're using a sponge from the kitchen or bathroom, make sure the sponge is thoroughly rinsed before you use it on plants—you don't want any chemical residue left on the sponge.

## 263

# Grow microgreens with the paper towel trick.

Microgreens are the super nutritious young sprouts of common vegetables like broccoli or beets. You can grow microgreens in soil, or you can skip the trouble of soil and use this method to grow them with only paper towels and water. From start to finish, it should take about a week to produce ready-to-eat greens, depending on the type of seed you're using.

## Materials:

- Microgreen seeds
- Paper towels
- Small tray with holes for drainage
- Drip pan

## Instructions:

1. The day before planting your microgreens, put the seeds into a small dish of water. Letting them soak overnight will help them sprout more quickly.

2. On planting day, fold a paper towel into at least two layers so it will fit nicely into the bottom of the tray. Soak the paper towel, then gently wring it out so it's moist.

3. Lay the paper towel in your planting tray.

4. Drain the seeds and scatter evenly across the paper towel. Set your smaller container onto the drip tray for drainage.

**5.** Cover the sprouting container with an additional damp paper towel and keep it in a dark place. The seeds should not be exposed to light.

**6.** Check your seeds daily—you might start seeing seeds sprouting as early as the first day. Mist daily.

**7.** The sprouts will grow quickly. Around the fourth or fifth day, when the first true leaves have emerged, move the container to a bright room so the sprouts can develop chlorophyll.

**8.** You can begin harvesting as soon as the leaves are green.

# 264

## Start a sprout jar to enjoy sprouts all year long.

Alfalfa and mung bean sprouts are crunchy, delicious, and packed with powerful nutrients. They're also really easy to grow yourself with a few basic supplies, including a wide-mouth jar, cheesecloth, and the right type of seeds. Start with a few tablespoons of sprouting seeds, then add 2–3 tablespoons of water to the jar and cover the top with cheesecloth and a rubber band. Let the jar sit out overnight. The next day, drain the jar by tilting it over a sink with the cheesecloth still in place. Add some more fresh water, swirl to rinse the seeds, and drain again and add fresh water. Repeat rinsing and draining your sprouts twice a day while the seeds crack and the sprouts begin to grow. You can harvest within a week.

# 265

## Keep your holiday poinsettias as houseplants.

Poinsettias are not only a beloved sign of the holidays; they are also one of the bestselling plants in the United States. Unfortunately, most poinsettias are discarded within weeks of being bought. If you want to keep your poinsettias alive for next season, follow these simple steps:

- After the flowering bracts (leaflike structures under a flower) are done, move the plant to a bright, protected place and keep watering.

- In the spring, trim your poinsettia, cutting several inches from the branches and reducing watering so the plant lightly dries out.

- In early summer, resume regular watering and fertilizing. If it's possible, move the plant outside, but avoid direct sunlight.

- In early fall, before the frost comes, move the plant back inside.

- In early October, begin providing the plant with 12 hours of uninterrupted, complete darkness every night. This will force it to rebloom so you can enjoy it during the holiday season.

## 266

### Spray plants with lemon juice or cayenne pepper to discourage pets.

As much as we love our pets, no one likes it when a kitten decides your prized vine looks delicious, or your puppy gnaws on your potted indoor tree. First, try to keep your pets away from your plants by keeping them in closed rooms. If you're still having trouble with your pets destroying your houseplants after that, try this simple trick. Mix up a spray of one part lemon juice to one part water and spray your plants with it. (Bottled lemon juice is fine for this.) If that doesn't work, stir some cayenne pepper into the mix. As with any spray, it's best to test this on a few leaves first to make sure it won't hurt your plants.

## 267

### Root your celery stem instead of tossing it.

Celery is not known for its long shelf life. Next time, instead of tossing your old celery, try planting the stalk and regrowing your own. For this to work, you need to save the entire root end of the celery bunch; planting a single celery rib won't work. Trim the celery ribs away from the root end, leaving about an inch. Set the root in a shallow dish of water. Put the dish in a bright place and change the water every few days. You should see new foliage emerging from the top, followed by new celery stalks. Harvest these when they reach a few inches in height.

# 268

## Create a kokedama, a hanging ball of ivy or vine.

*Kokedama* balls were invented in Japan as a really novel and beautiful way to grow certain plants. The word *kokedama* literally translates into "moss ball," which perfectly describes these decorative plant holders. Traditionally, *kokedama* balls are made with a heavy clay base. These balls, however, are created from regular potting soil and sphagnum moss.

### Materials:

- Potting soil
- Sphagnum moss
- Plant (ivy, bromeliad, orchid, or any small-foliage plant)
- Twine

### Instructions:

1. Prepare your soil mix and working area (outside if possible; this is a messy process). For the soil mix, mix the potting soil and shredded sphagnum moss in a 1:1 ratio.

2. To create the ball, load a few cups of the soil mix into a container and add water. Continue adding water and mixing by hand until the mix can be easily gathered and compacted into a solid ball.

**3.** To plant, carefully split the ball in half and lay the halves on a working surface.

**4.** Remove the plant from its container and gently knock away most of the dirt from the roots.

**5.** Lay the plant on one half of the *kokedama* ball, then put the halves back together and compress to re-form the ball.

**6.** Lay the ball with the plant upright in a pile of wet moss and gather up as much moss as possible to surround the ball, compressing as you go.

**7.** Gently tie the twine around the top of the ball, holding the plant in place, then wrap the ball thoroughly with twine to form a compact ball.

**8.** Display the finished *kokedama* ball in a dish, or hang it from a wire hook.

**9.** To water, soak the *kokedama* ball in a dish of water. Keep the moss wet by spritzing it daily or as needed.

# 269

## Make a DIY hover garden for trailing succulents.

Resembling lush UFOs, hover gardens are shallow, hanging gardens stuffed with bright succulents. You can easily create your own hover garden. The key is finding the right saucer—you want something wide and relatively shallow. Drainage holes aren't necessary. Start by laying down a bed of pea gravel, then a layer of moist cactus-potting soil. (If you can't find cactus-potting soil, add some perlite to regular potting soil.) Plant your succulents. Add trailing succulents like string of tears or burro's tail near the edges and taller cacti in the middle. Hang your hover garden in a bright spot and water it carefully, making sure to never let water collect in the bottom of the tray.

## 270
### Start your tulips in water early for spring blooms.

In many parts of the world, tulips are synonymous with spring and early summer. Grown in masses of color, these beautiful bulbs lie dormant all winter only to explode with foliage and blooms in March and April (depending on the type of tulip and your location). If you just can't wait that long for blooms, there's hope. Tulips readily sprout in plain water. To sprout a tulip bulb early, put a few inches of decorative gravel in the bottom of a tall, narrow tulip vase. Push bulbs down into the gravel and add enough water to submerge the bottom of the bulb. Check the water level daily to make sure the bulbs are continuously wet. When the bulbs sprout and begin to grow and flower, continue adding water to keep the plants nourished.

## 271
### Add dried grass to your plant groupings for a nice background.

One of the goals of displaying plants is to bring texture, variety, and character to your home. This simple trick makes it possible to bring the great plains inside—or at least make it look like you did! All you need are some bunches of dried grass or bamboo and a deep container so they can stand upright. Mix these grasses or bamboo into your plant collection. The brown stalks will complement your living display, exactly like tall grasses in your outside garden add interest and texture to your yard. Better yet, dried grass never needs to be watered or fed.

# 272

## Create an onion tower for never-ending green onions.

Onion towers are more than just a year-round source of fresh green onions...they're also incredibly cool and guaranteed to get noticed. Better yet, they're very easy to create with just a few basic supplies.

### Materials:

- Wide, large plastic bottle, like a juice bottle
- Wire cutters
- Wire hanger
- Pliers
- Potting soil
- 12 small to medium onions, any type

### Instructions:

1. Cut the top off the bottle.

2. Use the wire cutters to cut a length of the hanger off, then bend it to form a loop on one end about the size of the onions you're planting.

3. Mark planting holes on the container. You want three rows of four holes. Stagger the holes so the onions have room to grow. Poke several small holes in the bottom of the container for drainage.

**4.** To make the planting holes, hold the wire with pliers and heat the loop end of the wire hanger until it's hot, then use the hot wire to melt through the plastic bottle and create a hole.

**5.** To plant, fill the container with soil up to the first line of holes. Lay four onions on the soil, with their growing ends sticking out of the bottle. Push each onion into the hole from the inside to help prevent leaks.

**6.** Continue adding soil and onion layers until all the onions are planted and the container is full.

**7.** Put the tower on a tray and water gently. Move to a sunny spot.

**8.** After the onions sprout, rotate the tower daily. You can harvest the green onion sprouts as fast as they grow— your onion tower will continue to produce green onions for months.

## 273

### Steer drafts away from your plants with vent covers.

Do you have trouble with your houseplants getting brown leaf tips or edges? This common problem can be frustrating because it's hard to fix and it leaves your plants looking less than perfect. In most cases, this is caused by lack of humidity and cold air—often thanks to heating and cooling vents blowing directly on your plants. While you can (and should) be misting your plants regularly, you can also take steps to redirect that air away from your plants with simple vent covers. You won't lose any efficiency in your heat or AC, but your plants will thank you.

## 274

### Stop fertilizing in the winter to save money.

Even indoors, your plants experience natural growing seasons. In winter, when light levels are lower and it's cooler, many plants slow their growth or stop growing entirely. When this happens, their nutritional requirements go down a lot because they aren't putting energy into actively growing. So, to save some money in the winter, cut back on the fertilizer or even stop fertilizing entirely. This is especially effective if you're using liquid fertilizer, which can be expensive. Resume fertilizing at the first sign of spring as your plants wake up for the next growing season.

# Chapter 5

# TOOLS, PESTS, AND HARVESTING

# 275

## Discourage pests with coffee grounds.

It turns out that some garden pests hate coffee as much as you love it. In particular, slugs and snails will avoid coffee grounds, as will fleas. If you make a lot of coffee, start saving the grounds and adding them to your soil to discourage soilborne pests. (Grounds also attract beneficial worms.) And it gets better: While you're discouraging pests, you'll also be killing two birds with one bean: Coffee is loaded with nutrients that are good for plants.

# 276

## Grow ladybug-friendly plants to fight pests.

Ladybugs have a well-earned reputation for being the gardener's friend. These bright little beetles eat all manner of garden pests and don't cause any damage to your plants. It's possible to buy ladybugs online and release them into your garden, but unless your garden is surrounded by a net, there's no guarantee they'll remain where you want them. A better idea is to plant things that attract (and keep) ladybugs in your garden. Not only will this encourage the ladybugs; it's also cheaper than buying live insects. Some of the plants that attract ladybugs include butterfly weed, herbs like dill and cilantro, tickseed, and yarrow.

## 277

### Store your tools in a bucket of sand and treat with mineral oil to prevent rust.

An ounce of prevention is almost always better than a pound of cure, and that goes for your tools too. In this case, your "ounce of prevention" is actually an oily mix of mineral oil and sand that you can use to protect and store your tools. Start with a large container like a 5-gallon bucket or a plant container with no drainage hole. In a wheelbarrow, mix together playground sand and mineral oil until the sand is noticeably oily and the mineral oil is distributed throughout the mix. Fill the container with the mix and store it in a protected place (move the bucket into position before you fill it up, so it's not too heavy). When you're done working in the garden, wipe your tools clean and shove them blade-side down into the sand mixture. This will help keep them clean, and the mineral oil will keep them lubricated and protected from rust.

## 278

## Use the apple-in-a-bag trick to help your tomatoes ripen.

Vine-ripened tomatoes are the goal, but sometimes you'll have no choice but to pick your tomatoes before they're fully ripened. The good news is that tomatoes continue to ripen after you pick them, thanks to a gas called ethylene, which ripens tomatoes and other fruits and is emitted by ripening fruit. If you have a few green tomatoes you want to ripen more quickly, try folding them into a paper sack with a ripe apple. Apples (along with bananas and avocados) give off lots of ethylene, which will help your tomatoes make the trip from green to red. Check your tomatoes every day—you'll know your tomatoes are ripe when they have a distinct tomato smell.

## 279

## Use vinegar to clean rust from old garden tools.

We ask a lot of our garden tools, so it's only natural to give back to them when we can. Over time, with heavy use, even the sturdiest and highest-quality tools will rust. Fortunately, there are good home remedies to remove rust and restore your tools. One of the best is plain white vinegar. If you have a rusty tool, submerge it in white vinegar for 30 minutes, then remove it and scrub off the rust with a stiff brush. Very rusty tools might need longer in the vinegar bath, or they might need more than one trip into the bath to get fully clean. After the rust is removed, thoroughly dry the tool and apply a thin layer of mineral oil to protect it from future moisture damage.

## 280

### Repurpose an old pallet into a tool organizer.

Pallets are the sturdy wooden platforms used in the shipping industry to carry and move heavy stuff. Designed so the tines of a pitchfork can easily slide into the pallet, there are many uses for old pallets—and because they're mass-produced for shipping, used pallets are usually not expensive. You can sometimes pick them up from shipping companies for $10 each. In the garden, old pallets make excellent tool organizers. Creating your custom tool organizer is as simple as planning what tools you want to hang, then screwing hooks or clamps onto the pallet. You can paint the pallet first if it's going to be visible. When you're done, hang your new tool organizer and enjoy easy access to your tools.

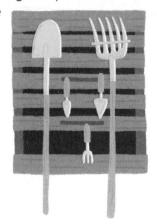

# 281

## Create a deer clacker to scare away deer.

Known in Japan as *shishi odoshi*, these fountains are made from bamboo that slowly fills with water until it tips over and empties with a loud *clack* into a basin. Some types can be complicated to make, but this version is a simpler option.

### Materials:

- Length of bamboo, up to 3" thick and at least 6' long, plus a 1" piece about 2' long
- Power drill
- Long bolt for metal axis rod (10" long)
- Basin
- Submersible pump
- Clear plastic tubing

### Instructions:

1. Cut a 3' length of the 6'-long bamboo, then cut one end diagonally to form the water scoop.

2. Create the scoop supports by burying two pieces of bamboo cut from the leftover longer piece, leaving a 3½" space between them.

3. Drill holes through both upright scoop supports, then drill a hole through the scoop about one-third of the way down the length of it. Using the long bolt, fasten the scoop between the supports. Leave the assembly loose enough that the water scoop can swing freely. When empty, the scoop should swing upright.

4. Position the basin beneath the scoop. Drill a hole for the pump electricity in the bottom of the basin.

5. Position the submersible pump in the basin.

6. Create the spout by burying another piece of longer bamboo, also cut from the leftover bamboo, at the edge of the basin and fastening the 1" piece of bamboo at the top, slightly angled down so water will flow out. Make sure the spout is positioned exactly over the opening on the water scoop when it's fully upright.

7. Drill a small hole in the base of the 1" bamboo piece.

8. Run the clear plastic tube from the submersible pump up the spout support and into the 1" bamboo piece.

9. When you turn on the fountain, water should flow from the basin through the spout and gradually fill up the water scoop. When the scoop is full, the weight of the water will cause it to swing down and loudly hit the rim of the basin while it dumps its water out. Once empty, the water scoop arm will swing back up and the process will repeat.

## 282

### Use a 5-gallon bucket as an easy tool caddy when you're gardening.

Carrying garden tools around is no fun, and wearing anything other than a simple pair of snippers on your belt weighs some people down. The solution is to create a portable tool caddy—but keep it simple! All you need is a 5-gallon bucket you can fill with snippers, shears, loppers, and other hand tools, then carry it around with you. Gone will be the days of losing your snippers in long grass because you set them down, or trudging back to your garage or garden shed to retrieve your forgotten tool.

## 283

### Make DIY slow-release fertilizer balls.

Slow-release fertilizer balls are popular among gardeners who grow a lot of hanging plants. These tidy little packets can be suspended above epiphytes like orchids or certain ferns, or tied onto your hanging flower baskets. Once in place, they'll provide a steady supply of food with even watering. To make your own, you'll need old pantyhose or an inexpensive new pair, some slow-release fertilizer, and string or monofilament line. Cut the pantyhose into squares about 4" on each side. Put 1–2 tablespoons of fertilizer pellets in the center of each square, then gather them up into pouches and tie them shut with string or monofilament line. Hang the balls above plants where they'll come into contact with water from your watering can or hose, so the pellets will slowly dissolve as the plant is watered.

## 284

## Create your own safe pesticide.

Every gardener has to deal with pests. Some of the most common include sucking insects like aphids, scale insects, mealybugs, thrips, and whiteflies. If you're battling bugs, the best strategy is to reach for the least-toxic option first instead of employing harsh chemicals right away. If spraying bugs away or wiping them off doesn't work, mix up a batch of homemade, nontoxic, organic pesticide, like this one based on a time-tested recipe from the now-defunct *Organic Gardening* magazine. In a blender, combine a whole garlic bulb with a small onion, 1 tablespoon of cayenne pepper, and 1 quart of water. Blend until smooth, then let the liquid steep for 5 hours. Strain it through a cheesecloth, then add 1 tablespoon of unscented dish soap. You can use this spray indoors or outdoors.

## 285

## Plant mosquito-repellent plants to keep bloodsuckers at bay.

Few things can ruin a relaxed evening in the garden or on the porch like hordes of mosquitoes. Not only do these annoying insects cause itchy bites; in some cases they can also carry disease, like the Zika virus. If you live in an area with mosquitoes, give your mosquito spray and citronella candles a boost by also including plants in your garden that drive away mosquitoes, such as lavender, marigolds, catnip, and geraniums. Herbs like basil and rosemary also work, and of course, you can plant citronella grass itself.

## 286
## Spray tools with isopropyl rubbing alcohol to clean them.

Using dirty tools is a good way to spread infection and pests among your plants—but washing tools between every use, or even between different plants, is an annoying and time-consuming job. Here's a quick tip: Keep a spray bottle of isopropyl rubbing alcohol near your gardening tools. A few quick sprays of alcohol on your tools, followed by a short wait, will go a long way toward ensuring you're not transferring fungi, bacteria, and even viruses among your plants. As a side bonus, rubbing alcohol can also make a good insecticide if you happen to see scale or other pests attacking your plants.

## 287
## Store commonly used tools in strategically placed pouches.

Spending time in the garden means reaching for snippers on a regular basis to snip off a dead flower here or trim back a runaway sucker there. Keeping your tools close at hand makes it easy to keep your garden looking crisp. This simple approach can help you hide tools in out-of-the-way or unexpected places, like inside cabinets, behind shelves or walls, or even under tabletops. First, either find or make a pouch or holster for your favorite tool, then glue or sew Velcro backing onto the pouch. Fasten another piece of Velcro to the surface so you can stick the pouch in place. Next time you need a tool, just grab it from your hidden pouch and snip away.

# 288

## Repurpose old wash bins or containers as hose hiders.

Hoses are vital to a healthy garden, but hoses lying all over the ground can be an eyesore. Various manufacturers sell different hose caddies and organization systems, but there's really no reason to spend money on a hose organizer that is actually just a large container. If you have any large circular containers around, like a wash tub or even a large plant container, you can easily press it into service as a hose container. If you don't, you can probably pick up something decorative and interesting from a thrift shop at a fraction of the cost of a new hose caddy. If your caddy is outside and exposed to the weather, just remember to get one that has drainage holes so rain can escape instead of filling up the container.

## 289

# Use your old tarps to make cleanup easy when deadheading or trimming.

Trimming your plants is often the easy part—things don't get hard until it's time to rake and bag or haul away all that debris. This quick trick takes some of that work away: Use an old tarp or blanket to collect your trimmings and deadhead flowers. Spread the whole tarp out, making a big target as you throw clippings behind you. When you're done, or when the pile is getting too big to manage, wrap the tarp into a bundle and shake it out directly in your compost bin or yard waste bag. Use this hack, and you won't have to rake the yard when you're done to clean up all the little bits of trimming left behind.

## 290

# Prevent fungus on your plants with cinnamon.

Vegetable gardeners already use cinnamon to protect their seedlings, but it doesn't have to stop there. There are many high-quality studies showing that cinnamon has powerful antifungal properties and that it's nontoxic. If you are worried about fungi attacking your plants and don't want to turn to a more powerful chemical, you can mix up an antifungal spray with cinnamon. Start with a quart of warm water and mix in 5 tablespoons of cinnamon. Let the mixture sit overnight to steep, then strain the liquid into a spray bottle. This spray is safe to use directly on plants.

## 291

### Protect your knees with sports knee pads while gardening.

Gardening is good exercise, but spending a day planting and weeding can also be hard on the knees and joints. If your knees ache from hours crouched over a bed of flowers or veggies, take this tip from professional tile installers: Use knee pads. A simple pair of sports knee pads, like the kind commonly sold for skateboarding, will take the pressure off your knees and reduce the strain of kneeling for longer periods. As always, however, if you're experiencing shooting pains or pain that doesn't resolve itself, make sure to check in with your doctor!

## 292

### Use diatomaceous earth to discourage slugs and snails.

Diatomaceous earth is the preserved skeletons of tiny organisms called diatoms. This naturally occurring substance is mostly silica and is used for a variety of applications, including pool filters...and deterring slugs and snails. The tiny crystals in diatomaceous earth are painful for slugs and snails to crawl across. Applying a thick layer of diatomaceous earth to the ground around your plants will create a deterrent, as the slugs and snails will avoid contact with the painful material. When handling diatomaceous earth, always follow safety instructions on the label—the same crystals that drive away slugs are also a possible lung irritant.

# 293

## Transform old denim jeans or shorts into an apron or garden tool belt (no sewing!).

Here's a clever hack that makes it easy to carry all the tools you need when you're working outside. Take an old pair of jeans and first cut the legs away, then cut down the sides to separate the front and back. That's it! You can wear the backside of the jeans like an apron, secured in place with a belt, and store tools or materials in the pockets. You can also hang more tools from the belt loops. If you're handy with a sewing machine, you can sew on a border to hide the cut seam or add more pockets from the leftover fabric. Best of all? When you're done gardening, you can throw your garden apron into the washing machine.

## 294

## Plant in bottomless plastic containers in the ground to ward off nematodes.

Nematodes are a type of worm that burrows through the soil and eats plant roots. Because they're underground, nematodes are very difficult to spot until your plants begin to show damage and slow growth. You can tell if a plant has suffered a nematode attack when you pull it up: The roots will have knobs where the nematodes have attacked. Unfortunately, it's very hard to control nematodes once your soil is already infected. This trick uses a simple barrier to discourage and slow down the nematodes, hopefully giving your plant time to grow and flourish before they cause serious damage. All you need to do is bury your plants in their original plastic containers with the bottoms removed, making it a little harder for nematodes to reach your roots.

## 295

## Use vinegar as a natural herbicide.

Herbicides are controversial chemicals, so many gardeners are uncomfortable using strong herbicides around kids and pets. If you're worried, skip the store-bought herbicides and use straight vinegar instead. Vinegar is a surprisingly effective herbicide for smaller, young weeds and weeds growing in cracks between pavers or in driveways. Spray the plants completely with a standard white vinegar and wait a few days. Reapply every few weeks if necessary.

# 296

## Set up a scrap bucket under your sink to make composting more convenient.

This commonsense trick solves one of the biggest obstacles to successful composting: inconvenience. A good compost pile usually includes a variety of vegetable and kitchen scraps, which means saving those scraps and carting them outside to your compost pile or bin. This simple, free hack makes it easy and convenient to collect those scraps—all you need is a small bucket or pail with a lid. Keep this under your sink, and throw scraps, eggshells, and other compostable waste into the bucket throughout the day. Keep it covered, both to contain smells and to discourage fruit flies or other pests. At the end of the day, just make one trip outside to add your scraps to your composter.

# 297

## Bury your rabbit fence deep enough to keep out burrowers.

It can be shocking how much damage rabbits can cause to a garden. Plants especially targeted by rabbits include tulips, lettuces, beans, berries, apples, and a wide range of trees. Rabbit fences are a good deterrent, but if you want to get your money's worth from a rabbit fence, make sure the fence is buried 12" deep. Rabbits are efficient burrowers and have little problem digging under shallow fences. If you want to keep them out for good, remember to dig.

## 298

### Contact your local agricultural extension office for advice and help.

All gardening is local—so wouldn't it be nice to have a local expert on hand to accurately answer any questions you have? In fact, you probably do. Almost every county in the United States has what's called an extension office. These offices are usually created in partnership with local universities and specialize in understanding agriculture and horticulture in your county. County extension offices are great resources for information on local plants, climate, soil types and conditions, and pests and problems. Many extension offices offer gardener hotlines staffed with master gardeners or county employees who have been trained to help with everything from identifying garden pests and insects to picking native plants for your landscape.

## 299

### Keep neem oil on hand to prevent a host of problems.

Neem oil is close to a miracle drug for your garden. Derived from the neem tree, native to India, neem oil has an extraordinary range of benefits for plants. It's a broad-spectrum insecticide that controls many of the most common pests in plants, and it's also effective against plant diseases and fungal infections. Neem can also be used as a foliar spray or soil drench. Finally, there is some evidence that neem can help your plants grow more quickly by making nitrogen more available in the soil. Neem is also safe and organic, so when used properly, it won't harm animals or children. You can find inexpensive neem oil in most garden centers and big-box stores, or you can buy it online.

# 300

## Make your own essential oils from homegrown herbs.

There are two main ways to make DIY essential oils. The first is oil infusion, which means putting the herbs in a high-quality oil and letting them steep. The second type is steam distillation, which sounds hard but is actually easily accomplished with a slow cooker. Here's how.

### Materials:

- 3–4 cups chopped fresh herbs, such as lavender
- Slow cooker

### Instructions:

1. Place the herbs in the slow cooker with enough water to fill it about two-thirds full.

2. Turn on the hot setting for 15 minutes to heat the water up, then reduce the heat to low and cook for 4 hours. If the water begins to evaporate, add more.

3. After 4 hours, let the mixture cool, then move the slow cooker container to the refrigerator for 24 hours.

4. Remove the container from the refrigerator. There should be a thin, hard layer on the top of the water. This is the extracted essential oil.

5. Carefully and quickly remove this layer and put it into a colored glass container. It's now ready to use!

## 301

## Keep a photo record of your plant labels in an album on your phone.

Over time, even the most durable plant tags fade with exposure to sun and water, making it impossible to read what type of plant is in the container. If you have just a few plants, this isn't a big deal—but if you have a collection of dozens, it can be frustrating not having the information from the tag. The solution to this problem is surprisingly simple and probably in your pocket or purse right now: When you buy a new plant, take a picture of the plant, and then take a close-up of the tag. Organize these pictures into an album. A year later, after the tag has faded, you'll have a photographic record of everything you own right at your fingertips.

## 302

## Use your leaf blower to blow away pests.

Along with water, air is the ultimate in organic pest control. For some types of pests, instead of any chemical control, all you may need to do is regularly blow them away. This works especially well to control populations of beetles and other slow-moving insects. First thing in the morning, hit your plants with a leaf blower to blast off Japanese beetles, earwigs, and potato beetles while they are still sluggish from the night before. Spreading a sheet on the ground before you blow pests away can make it easy to collect any bugs that fall off the plant, then discard them in a bucket full of water.

# 303

## Preserve your fresh herbs in frozen herb blocks.

When your herbs are ready to harvest, they're ready to harvest whether you need them or not. If you end up with more herbs than you can use quickly, there's a great way to preserve them for later use. First, chop the herbs roughly, then mix the chopped herbs with olive oil. Fill a standard ice cube tray with the herb and oil mixture, adding more herbs and oil to each cube to fill it up. Then freeze. Your frozen herb and oil blocks will stay fresh for months.

**Tip:** If you measure the amount of herbs and oil included in each block, you'll know how many cubes you need to thaw for any particular recipe.

## 304

## Make a DIY pheromone trap to kill pests.

Pheromones are specialized chemicals produced by insects and other animals to signal mating. Although they can't be smelled by humans, pheromones are highly attractive to their targets—insects can't help following their "noses" to discover the source of pheromones. You can put this to work against your garden pests by making a DIY pheromone insect trap. First, you'll need to buy pheromone lures or capsules from a garden supply store, along with a sticky insect-trap coating. To make your trap, cut a few holes in the side of a container, then paint the bottom of the container with the sticky coating. Hang the pheromone lure or capsule from the top of the container, then hang the finished trap in your garden. Insects will enter the trap through the side holes, then get stuck and die. Your new trap should last all season.

## 305

## Make DIY insecticidal soap.

Insecticidal soaps have been around for decades in the organic gardening community. These simple products—basically a formulation of simple soap—work by attacking soft-bodied pests like aphids and mealybugs, causing them to dehydrate and die. You can buy insecticidal soap, but you can easily make your own as well. Mix 3 tablespoons of unscented dish soap into 1 gallon of water and stir to combine. Because soap can damage some plants, test your spray on a few leaves first and wait a few days before using on the whole plant. To make your spray more effective, stir in mineral oil or vegetable oil.

# 306

## Check your plants at night (with a flashlight) to catch night marauders.

No gardener wants to wake up to a ravaged vegetable patch, but unfortunately some of our worst pests—including slugs and snails—do their dirty work under cover of darkness. If your garden is being damaged at night, you can stage a night counteroffensive with a flashlight and plastic bag. After dark, head out to your garden and look for the telltale slime trails. Inspect your plants closely, making sure to look under the leaves. If you see any slugs or snails, pluck them off with the bag and discard them. If you're worried they'll escape, you can sprinkle a little table salt into the bag to kill them.

# 307

## Install UV light traps in your garden to get rid of moths.

Flies, moths, and mosquitoes are more than annoying—they can spread diseases to your plants, and moth larvae are highly destructive. If your outdoor areas are overrun with flying night pests, instead of reaching for a chemical, consider installing a UV light and glue boards. These pest-control devices rely on the fact that many insects are attracted to UV light, so the bugs will fly toward the light and then get stuck on the glue board. They work especially well in areas with high concentrations of flying bugs, like back decks with landscape lighting or pool areas.

## 308

### Create sticky boards to catch and kill garden pests.

Sticky boards have been helping us catch pests for as long as insects have loved sticky things. These little boards are great for localized pest control and can help reduce the population of moths and other burrowing insects. To make your own permanent sticky boards, use thin plywood boards or strips cut into sections about 6" long and 3"–4" wide. Paint them yellow to attract insects, then cover the boards with specialized stick coating—you can find this online or in garden centers. Position the boards near your plants and check them frequently. You can scrape off any insects you catch and repaint the boards as needed. Your pest boards should last for several years.

## 309

### Make your own tomato leaf spray to use as a pesticide.

Little-known fact: When Europeans were first introduced to toma-toes from the Americas, tomatoes were considered highly poisonous. There are a few possible explanations for this view, but one obvious one is that tomato leaves actually *are* poisonous. Tomato leaves contain toxic compounds that make them inedible for many pests. You can put these toxic compounds to work in a homemade pesticide known as tomato leaf spray. To make tomato leaf spray, chop 2 cups of tomato leaves, then cover them with water and soak for 24 hours. Next, strain the mixture through cheesecloth into a spray bottle and use it as a regular insecticide, thoroughly soaking your plants.

## 310

### Plant "trap crops" to distract and catch pests.

This may be the only time you'll *want* to attract pests to your garden. Trap crops are plants that are planted specifically to lure pests away from your more valuable plants. By providing preferred food for pests, you'll pull the pests away from your main crops and onto the trap crop—and then you can destroy the trap plant along with any bugs on it. If you try this, it's vital to destroy the trap crop before the pest has had a chance to lay eggs and multiply, so that you're not actually increasing the number of pests in your garden. Examples of good trap crops include nasturtium, dill, beans, and chervil.

# 311

## Bag your fruit on the tree to protect it from pests.

Fruit farmers always want to bring their best produce to market—in fact, blemished fruit is often rejected long before it gets to your local market. This means farmers have to use every trick in the book to protect their fruit. You can take a page from their playbook with this simple hack to protect your own developing fruit from insects and pests: Individually bag fruits while they're still on the tree. This works especially well with apples and peaches and doesn't require any special material, just a box of regular zip-top baggies. Zip a bag around each piece of fruit, then cut a corner off the bag so condensation can drain out. Keep your fruit bagged until harvest.

# 312

## Scatter crushed eggshells around and in your garden to prevent slugs.

Slugs and snails are particularly annoying garden pests; they do their worst work at night, making it hard to spot them and pick them off. Instead of rooting around at night with a flashlight or resorting to potentially toxic baits, try using crushed eggshells to deter them. Spread a thick barrier of crushed eggshells around the stems of your plants. The sharp shells damage the slugs' soft underbellies when they try to crawl over them. As an added benefit, as the eggshells slowly deteriorate, they'll add minerals including calcium to your garden soil.

# 313

## Create DIY ant traps.

Ants themselves don't usually harm plants—but that doesn't mean you want them in your garden. Ants are known to "farm" aphids, because aphids provide an important food source for ants in the form of a sweet excretion known as honeydew. The ants will actually carry aphids from plant to plant to increase the aphid population. To control ants, you can make your own DIY ant barriers designed for tables, shelves, and carts. First, take an aluminum pie plate and make a cut to its center, then continue to cut a hole in the center to approximately the size of your table or shelf leg. Trim off a few inches from the outside edge to make it more manageable, then slide the aluminum disc into place around the leg. Secure it with tape, elastic, a few screws, or glue, then fold the aluminum down into a downward-facing cone. Finally, paint the inside of the cone with sticky insect-trap coating.

# 314

## Kill slugs and snails with beer.

Slugs and snails don't just like the scent of your plants. It turns out these nasty plant eaters are also attracted to the thick, yeasty aroma of beer. If you have persistent slug or snail problems, try leaving a dish of beer out overnight to attract and drown these pests. Make sure the dish is at least 5" deep, and leave a 1" rim around the top, so they are sure to slip in and won't be able to climb out. This approach works best if you can change out the beer every morning, and only set the dish out when there's no rain to fill up the container.

## 315

### Blast away sucking insects with a hose before reaching for pesticide.

One of the cardinal rules of pest control is to reach for the least toxic option first—and what could be less toxic than water? If you find yourself battling infestations of sucking insects like aphids, mealybugs, or scale insects, before you reach for a pesticide, try your hose first. In many cases, a concentrated jet of water focused on these pests will blast them away. After treating your plant, wait a few days for any larvae to hatch, then inspect the leaves and do it again. Always make sure to look under the leaves when you're treating an infestation. This works best on plants with tougher leaves, so you don't damage the plant.

## 316

### Make aluminum foil mulch to deter ground pests.

Aluminum foil probably isn't the first thing you think of when you think about recycled garden supplies, but there are actually a surprising number of ways you can use recycled aluminum foil to help your plants. One of the easiest is to create aluminum foil mulch from your used kitchen aluminum foil. All you have to do is clean and shred the aluminum foil, then lightly mix it into the top layer of mulch or soil in your garden. Pests like slugs and snails will avoid climbing over it, while the glare will keep away some flying insects like aphids.

# 317

## Use tree bands on your fruit trees to protect them from sun damage and boring insects.

White tree bands are a common sight in professional fruit orchards. Growers use bands to discourage all sorts of climbing and creeping insects, and to protect their tree trunks from sun damage. You can use this same technique at home if you're having issues with caterpillars, slugs, or other pests climbing from the ground up into your fruit trees. One of the most effective "bands" is actually a mixture of latex paint and diatomaceous paint. You can paint this directly on the tree trunk, or you can wrap the trunk in cardboard first and then paint that.

# 318

## Construct DIY trunk bands on trees to control rats and mice.

Trunk banding for rats and mice is an entirely different thing than trunk banding to prevent climbing insects. Rats and mice are more than happy to jump over a painted trunk band. To deter these hungry fruit thieves, you need to break out the big artillery: sheet metal. To create an effective metal band that rats and mice can't just jump over, start with a 24" strip of sheet metal. Wrap the metal around the tree trunk snugly, but not so tight that the tree can't grow. To fasten the band in place, punch a hole in the sheet metal where the band overlaps and tie it together with wire.

# 319

## Harvest your own burn and cut ointment with aloe vera.

Some of the most popular plants are also highly functional, such as aloe vera. This succulent has been used for hundreds of years as a remedy for all sorts of ailments, from stomachaches to small burns and cuts. Better yet, aloe is incredibly easy to grow in a container. Like most succulents, it likes bright light and regular watering with excellent drainage. Let the soil dry out between waterings. When you need to use your aloe, snip off one of the fleshy leaves and split it open the long way. You can use the gel inside as-is, applying a thick layer to wounds and burns to help them heal.

# 320

## Leave your garden spiders alone!

Spiders have a bad reputation they don't really deserve, especially in the garden. In truth, spiders are voracious insect eaters and don't cause any harm to plants. As creepy as it might seem, if you start seeing spiders in your garden, that's a good thing, and you should leave them alone. You'll be relieved to know that most spiders are harmless, so you're in no danger. If you see a spider you suspect is dangerous, like a black widow or brown recluse, don't attempt to touch it, but instead take a picture and call your local agricultural extension office. Many seemingly dangerous spiders have actually been misidentified, so it's always a good idea to check before killing it.

# 321
## Leave snakes alone too, so they can get rid of garden pests.

Even if you don't love snakes, you might learn to like them—or at least tolerate them—when you think about how beneficial they are to the garden. While no snake harms or eats plants, they do eat the rodents, marauders, and insect pests that drive gardeners crazy. Smaller snakes feast on grasshoppers and other bugs that can wipe out your garden, while larger snakes make short work of the rats that wouldn't mind sharing your fruit or tomatoes. In most cases, snakes are also shy, avoid humans at all costs, and are harmless.

# 322
## Deter snails and slugs with copper.

Copper is a natural deterrent to slugs and snails. The metal works because the slime on slug and snail skin interacts with the metal, causing an unpleasant chemical reaction that feels like a tiny electrical jolt. Put this natural reaction to work by using copper edging or strips to deter slugs and snails from entering your garden. You can use copper-backed paper, wide-gauged copper wire, or copper stripping. Copper edging can be pricey, but if you highlight it as a garden feature, you'll be killing two birds (slugs?) with one stone and getting a beautiful edging that also deters slugs and snails. For a more economical approach, however, just surround the stems of individual plants with loops of copper wire.

## 323

## Read and follow all label directions on chemicals to protect your health.

Gardeners—even many organic gardeners—often use a variety of chemicals to encourage plants to grow, control insect and pest populations, and prevent or treat diseases. For your own safety and the safety of anyone who visits your garden, it's always a good idea to carefully read and then follow all safety measures for whatever chemical you're using. This includes using personal protection equipment like gloves and respirators or face masks. It's also good to keep in mind that a product isn't safe simply because it's organic. While organic-labeled products do have good safety records, they should still be used as intended and with appropriate safety precautions.

## 324

## Use ammonia to control aphids, scale, and thrips.

Besides its usefulness for cleaning floors, regular household ammonia is also an effective and inexpensive pesticide. It's been shown to help control aphids, scale insects, thrips, and whiteflies. To make your own ammonia insecticide, mix it with water in a 1:7 ratio of ammonia to water and spray it on your plants. As with other pesticides, test it on a small part of your plant first to make sure it won't cause any harm to your foliage.

# 325

## Use spikes made from plastic forks to fend off rabbits.

This clever hack is like creating a minefield for rabbits or other small pests like rats. Using a pack or two of plastic forks (or cleaned used versions), bury the utensils around your plants with the tines sticking up. The goal is to make it hard for bunnies to hop around comfortably, so keep your fork field dense and really pack in the spines. This is an especially good idea when your seedlings are just coming up in the spring and your garden is full of delicious sprouts. A good fork field can help buy your tender young plants enough time to become established.

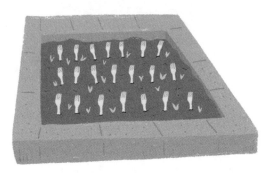

# 326

## Bring in beneficial insects with companion plants.

The assassin bug earns its name. These tiny winged insects are ferocious consumers of predatory insects...meaning that despite their fearsome name, these are insects you want in your garden. The same is true of lacewings, certain types of wasps, and many types of beetles. To encourage these beneficial pests, try adding a water source and places for them to live, and, above all, avoid large area sprays and chemicals that will kill them. The goal is to create a healthy population of beneficial insects that will contain outbreaks of true garden pests. To get a list of which plants are good companion plants in your area, call your county agricultural extension office.

# 327

## Hang red ornaments on vegetables to confuse and scare birds.

There are few things as frustrating as inspecting your fruit only to find holes pecked into your tomatoes or vines stripped clean by birds. Most experts recommend using bird netting to keep away flying bandits, but this isn't always practical and can be costly. Here's an easier and much less expensive approach—repurpose some old holiday ornaments into garden protectors. Birds are easily frightened and confused by things that move and make noise. Hanging a few red ornaments from your tomatoes will help discourage the thieves, especially after they peck at the ornaments a few times and realize they're nonedible.

## 328

### Rinse your harvest as you pick it to avoid getting a lot of dirt inside.

Harvest day can be a dirty job. To make the job go a little smoother, faster, and cleaner, here's a clever idea: Carry along a laundry basket (the kind with holes in the side for good airflow) and a bucket of clean water. As you're picking your vegetables, give them a plunge in the water to wash off most of the dust and dirt, then put them into the basket to dry. When you get the veggies inside, they'll already be prewashed and not covered in a layer of dirt.

## 329

### Spray isopropyl rubbing alcohol on leaves as an inexpensive pesticide.

Common isopropyl rubbing alcohol is an effective and inexpensive pesticide that works on a wide variety of insects. It works by dissolving the shells of insects and destroying their eggs, as well as drying out insects. Rubbing alcohol is usually sold in two strengths: 70 percent and 90 percent. You can use 70 percent directly as a spray to contain an active outbreak, or you can dilute it with water in a 1:1 ratio and use it as a preventive measure weekly. Before spraying rubbing alcohol on a plant, however, test it first on a few leaves to make sure it won't damage your plants.

# 330

## Disinfect your garden tools with bleach to prevent plant diseases.

Just like people and animals, our beloved plants are vulnerable to a wide range of diseases and problems. Blights, fungi, bacterial infections, and viruses can all disfigure or kill plants. To help prevent the spread of disease while you're working, make sure to disinfect garden tools with a common 10 percent bleach solution (meaning a 1:9 ratio of bleach to water). Soak your tools and other implements for 30 minutes. This will also lower the risk of spreading pests that ride along on your tools. Disinfecting is especially important for indoor or greenhouse gardeners—once a disease gets into your enclosed space, it can be very hard to control and may even require destroying plants.

# 331

## Spray baking soda on plants to prevent black spot and other fungal diseases.

Baking soda has well-documented antifungal properties. This non-toxic, safe product prevents black spot and powdery mildew and may be effective against existing infections. To create a baking soda spray, mix 1 teaspoon of baking soda into 1 quart of water, then add 1 teaspoon of an unscented dish soap and use a spreader that will help disperse the spray and thoroughly coat the leaves. Spray your plants weekly to prevent fungus, or treat existing outbreaks as needed.

## 332

# Make "bug juice" to discourage a wide range of garden pests.

"Bug juice" was one of the stranger ideas to gain mainstream attention in the 1960s—and that's saying something. Made from the pulverized and blended bodies of actual pest insects, this homemade spray is thought to scare bugs away from your plants. To make your own, collect about ½ cup of insects from your garden. Using an old blender (not one currently used for food prep!), combine the bugs with 2 cups of water and blend, then strain the liquid into a spray bottle and spray onto your plants. Because you're dealing with insects that might have been exposed to other pesticides or chemicals, always use protective mouth, eye, and skin covering when handling bug juice.

## 333

# Discourage deer with soap shavings.

Deer represent an adorable menace to gardens throughout the country. With deer populations exploding in suburbs everywhere, it's not uncommon to see half a dozen deer on an evening walk in some neighborhoods. And these large mammals are voracious eaters that can demolish a vegetable garden or hosta bed in a single morning. This simple hack uses deer's own finely tuned sense of smell against them. Deer don't like the scent of some soaps, especially Ivory soap. Spreading soap shavings throughout your garden will help discourage them. Just make sure to replenish the soap supply after every rain; and don't worry—the soap won't hurt any of your plants.

## 334

## Create a DIY bat box to attract insect-eating bats.

Bats are a welcome sight for many gardeners. These agile fliers take to wing every dusk and eat a huge number of insects—including insects that can damage your plants. One good way to attract bats to your garden is to include a special bat-roosting box. Luckily, they're inexpensive and easy to create. The best bat houses are thin and tall, with an open bottom and a rod or dowel for the bats to hang from while they're sleeping. Your bat house should be at least 15′ off the ground and ideally fixed to a building side or a pole in an area with plenty of access to sun. If you want to see specific plans for different types of bat houses, check out the Bat Conservation International website at www.batcon.org.

## 335

## Use sharp shears to harvest.

Wandering through your vegetable patch or berry rows, it can be tempting to sample the goods, popping off a tomato or strawberry to eat right there. While this is fine every so often, when it comes time to actually harvest, it's best to equip yourself with a sharp pair of shears when you head outside. Tugging or twisting fruit off the plant can easily damage the fruit, usually by peeling away a bit of skin where the stem is. The result is fruit and vegetables that don't last as long, as bacteria and pests exploit the wound.

## 336

### Cook your own garlic oil insecticide and antifungal treatment.

Garlic offers a host of powerful benefits. It kills bacteria and fungus, and it also works as an insecticide. This recipe for garlic oil produces a stronger spray than the water-based mixes, so be sure to test it on a small area of your plants before dousing your garden with it. To create garlic oil, mix 6–8 cloves of garlic, minced, with 1 tablespoon of mineral oil. Let it steep overnight, then add 2 cups of water and 3 tablespoons of unscented dish soap. Mix well and strain into a bottle to store. You can also add other ingredients, like cayenne pepper, to amp up the insecticide power of your spray. To use, mix 2 tablespoons of the oil concentrate with 2 cups of water and spray.

## 337

### Make your own herbal pesticide to save money.

Organic gardeners have long used herbal sprays to discourage insects—it turns out that many common garden pests dislike some of our most popular herbs just as much as we love them, especially rosemary, sage, and thyme. To create a completely organic herbal spray, chop up about 2 cups of herbs and mix with 2 cups of water and bring the mixture to a brief boil. Let it cool and then let the herbs steep overnight in the water. The next morning, strain the mixture and save the herbal spray. In addition to the herbs listed previously, you can also experiment with lavender, mint, nasturtium, and other herbs. The best recipe is the one that works for you!

# 338

## Create potato starch spray to kill pests.

Starch sprays—based on potato starch or even regular baking flour—work by gumming up the leaf surface so pests get stuck and suffocate. In past days, some gardeners would simply sprinkle flour on their plants. Today, you can make an effective starch spray using potato starch. Mix 4 tablespoons of starch into 4 cups of water, then add ½ teaspoon of unscented dish soap to help spread the spray and make it stick to the leaves. Spray your affected plant thoroughly, including the underside of the leaves. The starch may leave a white or gummy residue. You can rinse this off after three days, then re-treat the plant as needed.

# 339

## Clean up rotting and fallen plant material to discourage pests.

Good hygiene matters in your garden too! Many types of pests feast on dead and dying plant material. Removing fallen leaves, cutting off dying branches, and generally keeping your garden clean from rotting organic material deprives pests of a place to get a foothold in your garden. With fewer pests, you'll actually save yourself time and money working in the garden, and you won't have to use as many chemicals to control outbreaks. To make this job easier, try keeping a debris bucket in a strategic place, so when you're walking around the garden, you can pick up anything you see.

## 340

# Put a rain gauge on your sprinklers to reduce water use.

Water conservation is always smart gardening—and nothing uses water like a lawn with an automatic sprinkler system. If you're dealing with high water bills from your sprinkler, invest in an inexpensive rain gauge for your system. This device senses when it's raining and keeps the sprinklers off. You'll spend less money on watering your lawn, and your grass will still get the water it needs. This is a good idea even if you have a well—in many parts of the country, water shortages are a serious problem, so anything you can do as a gardener to save water is welcome.

## 341

# Don't harvest wet fruit or vegetables.

Plant blights like fungus and bacteria love damp—and they're always looking for a way to ruin your harvest. For best results on your harvest day, wait for a dry day, and don't harvest wet vegetables and fruit. Tramping through a wet garden, especially while you're harvesting vegetables and fruit and cutting into plants, is a good way to spread diseases. Harvesting on a dry day, by contrast, makes it that much harder for diseases to spread.

## 342

### Water your herbs thoroughly the day before picking them so they last longer.

Herbs are often harvested as they're needed, snipped away leaf by leaf. However, if you have to harvest herbs all at once and save them for a few days, here's a tip to prolong their shelf life: Water them thoroughly the day before. Ideally, you want to harvest herbs when they are at peak fullness and the leaves are plump with water. Water-stressed leaves will shrivel faster, ruining your herbs. If you must harvest herbs when they are a little dry, you can put the cuttings into water to plump them back up before you use them.

## 343

### Move your newly harvested fruits and veggies out of the hot sun right away.

Most vegetables and fruits appreciate being moved to a cool, dry location as soon as possible after you've cut them. Leaving freshly harvested fruit or vegetables in the sun hastens their spoiling and shortens their usable life. To get the most from your harvest, try getting your produce inside as quickly as possible. If you have an especially large vegetable patch, harvest it in stages, moving the crops into a cool, shady area as you go, then heading back out for more.

# 344

## Leave a little stem on your harvested fruits and vegetables.

Here's a good tip to make harvest easier and more manageable: When you snip away your fruits and veggies, leave a little bit of the stem intact. This will not only make them easier to handle; it will also protect them from injury related to skin tearing around the stem. The only caveat: Be careful not to let the stem bits poke holes in other produce as you load up your basket or bag with freshly picked fruits and vegetables. When you are done harvesting, you can leave the stems on until you're ready to prepare the produce for use.

# 345

## Pay attention to your plants!

The best thing you can do for your plants is also one of the simplest: Pay attention to them! Your plants may not talk or have tails to wag, but they are always communicating with you, so try to inspect them daily. A drooping leaf might signal your plant is thirsty. Speckling on leaves can indicate whiteflies or thrips are feeding on the underside of the leaf. Roots peeking up from the soil can mean it's time to repot your root-bound container plant. Spend time with your plants, and you'll find they'll grow even better.

# 346

## Use Bokashi composting for all kitchen scraps, including meat and dairy.

Bokashi, Japanese for "fermented organic matter," is a type of composting that originated in East Asia and uses a specialized inoculated bran and a closed-bucket system to compost organic matter. One of the main advantages to Bokashi composting is that it allows you to compost meat (including bones) and dairy. Also, Bokashi composting is much faster than traditional composting. If you're interested, it's best to start with a dedicated Bokashi bucket kit, which will include the inoculated bran. These buckets come equipped with a spigot that allows you to drain off the liquid that forms during composting. To start the process, fill up the bucket with kitchen waste mixed with the bran, then seal it tightly and move it to an out-of-the-way place for 10–14 days. At the end of the fermentation, everything in the bucket will be thoroughly fermented and can be added to your regular compost pile or dug into the garden to finish decomposing. Because Bokashi compost is so acidic, plant roots should not come into contact with the freshly fermented product for at least two weeks.

## 347
### Get rid of scale with cotton swabs and alcohol.

Scale is a persistent problem for many plants, partly because it can be very hard to control. Scale insects are covered with a hard shell that protects them from chemicals and sprays while they feast on your plants. If you have a bad outbreak, however, this hack is an inexpensive and effective way to control scale. Soak a cotton swab in 70 percent isopropyl rubbing alcohol and wipe away the scale. You can use Q-tips to reach into nooks and leaf junctions. When you're done, rinse the plant with a jet of water to remove any debris or dead bugs. Repeat the procedure after a week or as needed.

## 348
### Make your own horticultural oil to use as a pesticide.

Horticultural oil is an inexpensive, organic, and effective pesticide for sucking insects. The oil works by smothering the insects so they can't breathe, eventually killing them. The key with horticultural oil is to coat the whole plant, including the underside of the leaves. To create a batch of homemade horticultural oil, mix 1 tablespoon of unscented dish soap into 1 cup of oil. You can use soybean oil, canola oil, cottonseed oil, or mineral oil. Add 2 tablespoons of this mix to 1 cup of water, then shake vigorously to combine and use as a spray. For best results, apply weekly.

# GARDENING RESOURCES

The following resources are great places to get more information about some of the concepts covered in this book.

**American Community Gardening Association.** The ACGA is devoted to supporting community gardening across the country. Visit them here: www.communitygarden.org.

**American Horticultural Society.** The AHS was created in 1922 to share information on gardening and plants, with a focus on sustainable gardens. Visit them at https://ahsgardening.org.

**AHS Native Plant Societies.** Native plants can make gardening easy, and they're good for the environment. To see an index of native plant societies around the country, visit the American Horticultural Society's Native Plant Societies index here: https://ahsgardening.org/gardening-resources/societies-clubs-organizations/native-plant-societies/.

**AHS Plant Society Index.** If you're interested in a comprehensive listing of plant societies, you can use the AHS directory of plant societies here (organized by plant type): https://ahsgardening.org/gardening-resources/societies-clubs-organizations/societies-by-plant-type/.

**American Orchid Society.** The American Orchid Society is the definitive source for orchid information in the United States. Visit them at www.aos.org.

**Cactus & Succulent Society of America.** Cacti and succulents are some of America's favorite indoor plants. Learn everything you need to know about growing them here: https://cactusandsucculentsociety.org.

**Dave's Garden.** *Dave's Garden* is one of the largest online communities devoted to gardening and all things plants. Connect with other gardeners here: https://davesgarden.com.

**Farmers' Almanac.** Continuously published since 1818, the *Farmers' Almanac* is a gardening institution. The *Almanac* offers weather predictions, calendars, and advice on gardening. View it here: www.farmersalmanac.com.

**Garden Club of America.** This all-volunteer, nonprofit group was founded to unite the country's hundreds of gardening clubs. This is a great resource to get more connected to your local gardening community. Visit them at www.gcamerica.org.

**Herb Society of America.** The Herb Society of America is a resource for growing and using fresh herbs. Visit them at www.herbsociety.org.

**National Agricultural Library, Community Gardening.** Community gardening involves growing veggies on borrowed land, usually in urban areas. If you don't have access to your own growing space, this is a great resource for getting started with community gardening. Visit the USDA resource here: www.nal.usda.gov/afsic/community-gardening.

**National Gardening Association.** The National Gardening Association is one of the premier organizations offering gardening advice and community for gardeners. Check them out at https://garden.org.

**Old Farmer's Almanac, Cooperative Extension Services Directory.** County extension offices are great local resources for gardeners. To find a comprehensive directory of extension services, the Old Farmer's Almanac maintains an index here: www.almanac.com/content/cooperative-extension-services.

**Planet Natural.** Founded in 1991, Planet Natural is a comprehensive resource for information on organic gardening, both indoors and outdoors. Visit them here: www.planetnatural.com.

**Seed Savers Exchange.** The Seed Savers Exchange is devoted to preserving America's heritage plants and is a great place to discover new varieties of the plants you already love. Visit them at www.seedsavers.org.

**Square Foot Gardening Foundation.** For more information on how to get the most from your small space, check with the Square Foot Gardening Foundation at https://squarefootgardening.org.

**United States Composting Council.** The US Composting Council is devoted to all things composting. Visit them here: www.compostingcouncil.org.

# INDEX